# Diary of an Ex-Husband

My Pain Had A Purpose!

By: Michael McCain

# Diary Of An Ex-Husband

Although the author and publisher have made every effort to ensure that the information in this book was correct at press time, the author and publisher (Maximize Publishing Inc. & Dr. Michael McCain) do not assume and hereby disclaim any liability to any party for any loss, damage, or disruption caused by errors or omissions, whether such errors or omissions result from negligence, accident, or any other cause.

The names and identifying characteristics of certain individuals referenced in this publication have been changed. This publication contains the opinions and ideas of its author. Relevant laws vary from state to state. The strategies outlined in this book may not be suitable for every individual, and are not guaranteed or warranted to produce any particular results.

No warranty is made with respect to the accuracy or completeness of the information contained herein, and both the author and publisher specifically disclaim any responsibility for any liability, loss, or risk, personal or otherwise, which is incurred as a consequence, directly or indirectly, of the use and application of any of the contents of this book.

Maximize Publishing Inc.
2018 Monterey Ave
Bronx N.Y. 10457
Attn.: Michael McCain
C/o: Kevin Brown

# Diary Of An Ex-Husband

© 2014 by Maximize Publishing Inc. & Dr. Michael McCain Enterprises Inc.

For Author: Michael A. McCain

All rights reserved, including the right to reproduce this book Or portions thereof in any form whatsoever. Any Reproduction of this book in recording, print or otherwise is punishable by law and copy right standards. For any information or contact with the author you may write the above named address.

**ISBN-13:**
**978-0692224984**

**ISBN-10:**
**069222498X**

Diary Of An Ex-Husband

Diary Of An Ex-Husband

# Table of Contents:

From My Heart
Dedication & Acknowledgments
Why I Wrote This Book
Chapter One: Dairy Of An Ex-Husband
Chapter Two: It Hurts Like Hell
Chapter Three: The Big Announcement
Chapter Four: Trick or Treat?
Chapter Five: Every Man Has a Breaking Point
Chapter Six: Symptoms of a Marriage Breakdown
Chapter Seven: Marriage Infidelity
Chapter Eight: Infidelity & Stages of Recovery
Chapter Nine: Five Rules to Guide Marital Recovery
Chapter Ten: Emotional Epiphany

Diary Of An Ex-Husband

# From My Heart:

No part of this book is intended to harm or bring pain to my ex-wife or to our children. But it is time I break my silence and start to address some of the pain men go through from a marriage break up and infidelity. It's always assumed that when a marriage goes wrong or sour it's always the husband that takes the entire fault for the make or break of the relationship. I can also admit that I was not nor am I perfect to this present day, but the one truth I can stand on is that I did everything in my power to save my marriage and make my marriage right.

I did not decide to write this book in an effort of making my ex-wife look bad. It's not my intention to run her into the ground, but what I have done is shown examples from both my marriage and from couples I have worked with and counseled. The advice I am sharing in this book has helped couples heal and fix their marriage. In counseling sessions I have even saved a few marriages from break up because of my extensive insight in how men feel who are being cheated on, or who have relationships with promiscuous women. Likewise my advice in aiding women to understand what men want in a marriage and relationship; please take this advice and these words from my heart.

# Dedication

I dedicate this book to every man who attempted marriage and failed.
I dedicate this to every man who fought for their marriage and made it work.
I dedicate this book to every young man who will one day get married. I dedicated this work to every father, grandfather, son and brother.
I dedicate this work to the people who build up marriages and not tare them apart.
I dedicate this book to the brother who had his struggles but one day got it together.
I dedicate this book to the young man and old man who will read this book and change his life because of its contents.

# Special Appreciation

I especially want to thank my parents for sticking with me and standing with me before, during and after my divorce. I want to thank my brother Bruce, for lending his ear and advice, even when you think you went unheard. I want to thank my church family who prayed for me, when I couldn't pray for myself. I want to thank "the wise men", who I receive marriage counseling from that molded me into the man I am today. Some of those mentors have gone on, but your message lives on in my heart, thank you for your words of wisdom.

# Why I Wrote This Book

Diary of an ex-husband is a book for any man who has been married and survived a divorce or terrible marriage. No matter what stage of the game you may find yourself in diary of an ex-husband will hit home for many. I call it "A Man's Guide to Surviving Divorce." Once you have been in a real marriage it's hard to unwind yourself from that relationship no matter how long or short you have been in it. While I am not promising to hit every possible detail a person can experience in a bad marriage, my work with this book was first a healing process and mental clarification for myself. This book allowed me to step back, take a look at my life, assess the damages and decide to get in the business of family again.

This book also was my road through mentoring numerous couples who went through the same type of marriage if not worse than what I experienced. One thing that I give God all the glory for is keeping me, in all that I've experienced some life changing things, something's that would give people mental breakdowns that they don't come back from. I know it was God that kept and covered me from losing my mind and last but not least being a man who in rage took someone's life over things that was not worth it.

# Diary Of An Ex-Husband

This Diary of an Ex-Husband contains not just my life lessons, but examples, stories from people I've mentored and counseled and have grown and learned from the process of mentoring and helping others. The reason why I wrote this book is because I have a calling to reach people in my writing, people will read this book that I'll never be able to have a conversation with. This book will take legs and go into the homes, the minds, the hearts, and the lives of people I may never be able to touch personally. Yet through this work my message will be given to a people hurting and searching for answers to concerns that's ripping their lives to shreds.

Early on I learned to appreciate the gift of writing. From my tender years of life seven years old and straight into my teens I learned to use the art of writing and expressing myself with the pen to dump feelings that I could not control. Feelings I had no outlet for. Tell the stories that I was unable to tell anyone else. The problem here is that the story I am telling, many people do want to hear, some for positive reasons and others just for the sake of saying they know something personal about your life.

No matter why you have this book in your hands your understanding will transformed. You will be able to walk away with healthy tactics to a life changing situation that will both help you to get out and heal, but also to move on. If I do nothing else with my work in this book I want every man to walk way knowing that you can move on with life. It doesn't matter if you're at fault for the divorce or you were one that just never saw it coming. The truth is it's over now. You can heal, be empowered to heal and overcome by knowing you're not alone in the battle, others have faced some hard roads just like you and are transforming their lives through their experiences and so can you.

I did my best in this book to not compromise the integrity of people. I've altered the names of people in this book but all stories related to marriages and the people in this book are real and not made up. I am excited for every reader, I am sure this is one book that you will share with every married, single, divorced, and engaged man that you know.

Take this journey with me into life lessons from a sensitive place in my life and in the lives of people willing to share their stories with me. I know I may not have touched every issue that people may have wanted me to, but this book comes straight from the heart and not really designed to fit anyone's standard of what they think it should be. When something comes from the heart, it is an expression that the author puts out and looks at it as a master piece no matter if no one else sees it in that light. I am sure by the end of these pages you will agree this book was well worth taking the chance at being myself, and delivering the message the way "Michael" needed to tell it.

Enjoy-

# Diary Of An Ex-Husband

# Diary of an Ex-Husband

My Pain Had A Purpose!

By: Michael McCain

Diary Of An Ex-Husband

# Chapter One:

## Diary Of An Ex-Husband

*"If I failed at anything it was not love, I opened my heart and I tired. You can't love a person who has not learned to love themselves." Michael McCain*

It started when I hung the phone up, a very good friend of mine that I had not talk to for some time called me and was sharing with me some of his experiences in the past two years and a half that I could not imagine would be so. See, just like me we were young men growing up with passion for life that allot of young men our age didn't have, we were goal driven and family orientated young men, but very mature, it was often said that myself and some of my associates and friends were beyond our years. That night I must have talked with my friend Robert and encouraged him out of a deep place. See, we were both married at a young age, both owned our own businesses and had lots of influence in our community, but were married to women who were not ready.

Not ready, I learned in my young age that the success of a marriage really has nothing to do with age. People young and old get married and end in divorce. Some people wanted to say that it was our young age and being inexperienced at life that left us unprepared for the fortification a real marriage needed. Yet the truth holds that people come from all walks of life, having parents and grandparents who have had successful marriages and family lives but there's still end in divorce. The one lesson I made clear with myself was that my failed marriage wasn't even all my wife's fault, but it was the type of woman I was attracted to.

I want to first make it clear that my purpose for writing this book is not to dog my first wife and make her out to be nothing less than the truth of our experience. I will admit that I was not perfect myself but I fought with all my might to save a marriage that was headed for disaster. When I counsel and speak with other men I am telling them about life out of my own experience. Most people look at me and say you're too young and don't know enough, some of these same men would give up if they had to walk a block in my shoes!

While talking with Robert it just hit me like a ton of bricks that if I was going to both overcome what I experienced then it was time to find an outlet to get my story out. Even if it meant that my story was not to be told to masses but to a select people who would benefit from a man keeping it real on issues that we face. One thing that I must tell you is that men internalize things and don't talk about problems often. The one major mistake that winds up happening is when a man finally shares something it's with a Delilah whose ready to zap his strength and put her claws around his manhood hoping she can keep him whipped!

Just in case I didn't make it clear the first time I want to open this up by saying I am not a perfect man, but when I fell in love with my first wife I can tell you that just what it was, "I FELL!" While I was personally believing God at my young years of 17 years old to show me a perfect image of what my future would be like with a family, I started praying for a wife. I had gotten tired of dating female after female to find out that they were not the fit for me. I remember family members and friends would say I changed women like I did my draws. The truth was I didn't waste time in relationships that didn't add up to my standard. I would rather break your heart immediately then to wait and break your heart later by doing something crazy.

# Ready To Say I Do

I was young as they come when I got married, it was September 27th, 2004 and it felt like heaven. You couldn't shake the confidence that I had that I was on my way to building a family that was going to be a force to be reckoned with. As a matter of fact I was the second out of my three older brothers to be married. There were many factors that played into my reasons for wanting to be married and the number one and foremost on the list was that I was a young, fly and saved man. Already growing up in a broken family I had a million reasons why I didn't want to be like my family.

As a matter of fact my friend Robert could relate to me on every level of my personal beliefs and convictions because our lives mirrored each other so much it was scary.
See, I grew up in the foster care system of New York City and came out of care on my own, running away from my foster mother at the age of 14-15. I had been to jail for running away, not because I was a bad kid but that's what the system did with teens who run away from home. One day I decided to run away and never turn myself in like I would usually do.

There were times I spent many nights out on the street homeless, no place to go. Not wanting to go to anyone's house I knew because I didn't want the police looking for me. I lived out of a book bag, when I did arrive to a friend or family member's house it was long enough to eat, wash up and back to sleeping in the stair case of the building or walk the streets and find a 24hr. Laundromat to sleep in for the night. At the age of 16 I came back home to live with my biological family taking care of my parents and doing what I felt was right in spite of the fact these people should have raised me.

## Diary Of An Ex-Husband

It didn't matter that while I grew up as a young man I was depressed many nights while children went home to their brothers and sisters I was coming home to a foster mother who didn't understand my struggles. It was not that my foster mother wasn't a good mother or couldn't love me, it was that I came knowing that I had a real mother that I could not see, a father who I felt should be raising me. While children went home to their families I was coming home to strangers and some days finding out a new little boy or two was in my room that I now had to share this room with and tell people these strangers where my brothers.

No one knew what pain I was holding inside, when I was just a teen no longer able to deal with the struggle and juggling act of emotions I had no outlet for. Where was I supposed to express this? Who was going to listen? When would I find relief? God, became my outlet, church became my way of expression. Gaining influence through my talents and gifts in my community was how I dealt with the pain; people always told me when I sing it had so much feeling in it, when I preached I reached them right where they were. Problem was I felt like I just wanted to be loved by a people I belonged to.

When I returned home to my family, I had dated several girlfriends and none of them seem to be the right fit for me. Many of them loved me and the break up was really dreadful but I didn't want to linger in relationships that I knew were not for me. Not knowing I was heading for a marriage that would change everything about the way I looked at life and relationships. I prayed and asked God for a wife and here came this pecan skinned, long hair having woman, who whisked her way into my life and I fell in love.

I dated the young lady and shortly into the relationship I proposed wanting her to know that I was not like other men that she may have dated. I remember telling all my closest friends never to date women with children; it was a culture shock for my friends to see me so madly in love with a young woman with child. I had no fear over walking into a ready-made family, after 10 years of foster care and helping tend to other children my whole life, playing the big brother and protector I honestly felt like becoming someone's father at this point couldn't be too far off from the responsibility I've grown up with all my life.

So it was off to city hall, no wedding, just I do. I called a God-sister of mine and asked if she would come downtown with us to witness the marriage, she agreed and I was all set. I remember I had this eerie feeling after saying I do as if something dreadfully wrong had happen, but I just wrote it off as me being nervous and walking into a level of manhood now that I would have to get used to. So I settled my spirit by praying over it and leaving it alone after and embracing my new found marriage. It was out to dates and making sure I spend as much time as possible with my wife.

No time to hang out with the boys and friends like I would usually do, no more people calling my house whenever they felt like they wanted to. I was now a changed man and made people respect my marriage weather they wanted to or not. I was challenged by so many people, women who I would have loved to date all of a sudden wanted to express their interest in me now. It seemed like me being married now became an extra turn on and attention getter that I didn't have before. No matter what I felt like I had to maintain my boundaries but quickly learned that the level of respect I gave my marriage my wife had not learned that experience yet and didn't walk in that same integrity.

# Diary Of An Ex-Husband

# Chapter Two:

## It Hurts Like Hell

*"Life is like an onion. You peel it off one layer at a time, and sometimes you weep." Carl Sandberg-*

Many people say men don't cry, well I can tell you that it's a lie. I never sat around crying every day because my marriage was over, truth be told I was over the marriage before I made my decision to walk out of it. I lived for two years married to a woman who I had fell out of love with. I can tell you from both the experience and my pain that's one of the most dangerous things a person could do, fall out of love and stay in that relationship. You will only begin doing things to cope with your pain or to make the other person's life a living hell because of your pain. I can tell you today I did them both.

The pain of knowing you're in a marriage headed for divorce will make you mentally and emotionally sick. You can't think as clear as you would use to and the brighter day is a false hope you keep holding on to brainwashing yourself that things will get better. See I grew up in a God-fearing house hold were divorce was never in my vocabulary. In my understanding I watched my family go through hell and marriages and make it all work out and that's the faith I had for mine. No matter what I had to face I was going to make it work.

Most people would tell you that if your marriage is over, "just get over it and move on". Truth is if you marriage was over a year or more, five years, ten years, two years it doesn't matter. It's still a broken relationship between two people who came together in life. Sometimes people want you to throw away your experience as if it has not happen to you and tell you to move on. What I will say is… your hurt and pain is valid. Take your time to grieve and move on from there, don't live in that place. Some men have a tendency of kicking up their feet and making a bad place home once they have been through a rough spot. I know I was made to be a great husband and father to a family so why would I stop there?

One thing that helped me deal with my marriage was this, "I can't make someone love me", and I also "can't make someone be faithful". Once I gave up the responsibility of trying to make every wrong right, I got delivered from trying to defend something that was bound to fall apart. I can tell you I gave my marriage my whole heart, I was not perfect but I came at marriage with everything I had and was determined to be the best husband a woman could have. With this understanding I could not understand some of the events that unfolded later in my marriage that not only rocked my personal life but my social life as well. Over the years of being married many in my community had grown fond of us, we were a growing powerful couple in New York. Rubbing elbows with prestigious religious leaders and business men. Soon to find that from the beginning of my marriage I was married to a woman who was broken, full of low self-esteem, lust and pride. I have so much sympathy for my wife because how in the world could I judge when I was not perfect myself? The same love and compassion I was showing her, was just what I had received from God myself.

I remember the long nights walking the streets of the Bronx talking to God some nights, other nights it was talking to my best friend at the time Anthony who lived in Michigan. I would pick up the phone and dial my friends number sometimes can barely speak English belting out what I could in pain, thanking God for a friends who could understand my gibberish and the lack of sense my words would make at times. I would ask what should I do, knowing I am already married, didn't want to turn back, knowing I was willing to fight to make everything right but what do you do when you're married to a woman who has so much self-esteem that she sleeps around?

# Diary Of An Ex-Husband

What do you do when you're married to a woman that looks in the mirror every day and see nothing good about her-self, always telling her friends that "no man will ever want me or be able to deal with me". What do you do with a woman who has a 3 year old that you're raising as your own son because his father walked out and left them, you become the only father he knows. So what do you do after long evenings of counseling with the Pastor and coming out the meeting fired up and feeling like I can make this marriage work, waking up the next day to a woman walking through the door with another man's scent on her.

What do you do when modern technology has advanced beyond using laptops and desk tops and now we are texting people, hiding phone numbers in our Sims card on our phone and lying saying the person we are talking to is our "girl-friend". Do you know what it's like to question every person you see your spouse communicate with, the more you try to be trustful you know that she's nothing but lustful so lust has no boundaries and will do anything. You suck it all up because you don't want to bring up accusations so you deal with it inside. Yeah, that's only two percent of the torment that I was under.

There were days that I felt like it was not worth staggering onto another prayer line because the answer to my problem was already plain. I was in a war that I didn't feel like fighting. On one hand I was ready to fight for my family, then on the other hand my mind had not yet process all that I was experiencing and how was I going to bring about a change. The first thing I decided to do was love her in spite of the mess that was going on until I had a more sensible plan on what I was going to do. I never believe in making emotional decisions because they only make things worse.

# 5 Stages of Recovery

### "A fear faced is a fear erased."

There are five stages to the recovery process when trying to understand how to get over a divorce: denial, anger, bargaining, depression and acceptance. There are times when the cycles intermingle and overlap or even seem absent. It is unusual though for any one phase to be missed completely. I can tell you from my experience that I lived at every stage of the process until I found my way out.

No matter what stage of the game you're in accept the process, assess the damages and walk out in victory. Sometimes you feel like you have to walk out of something with more than what you came in with to feel like a winner, but if the truth be told sometimes you have to walk out with just your life and that means more than anything else. Relationships will strip you, drain you and when you're coming through the tunnel of a divorce you might walk out with just the clothes on your back but understand that you will make it and you will recover no matter where the pieces may fall.

## Diary Of An Ex-Husband

Before I give you the breakdown of the 5 stages of recovery let me explain something to women who maybe reading this book. This is not a women bashing book in no wise, but an honest and candid look into a life of an ex-husband who is real enough to pull other hurting men out of a rut and pit that some sister has put him in and put a lid on it. If I further tell the truth there are men reading this book that deserved the divorce but need to know where they went wrong, searching for answers on how to be a better man but don't have a mentor nor a voice to show them the way.

Some of us have played games in our adult lives and in our relationships and marriages; some of us have built up habits and desires that we find hard to break from. Sometimes people don't get tired of something until it's exposed and unable to be fixed.

If you are a brother with a good woman who's playing games, pimping and checking in with your women here and there, you still have a chance to come out and fix your life before it's too late. If that's the reason why your divorced today that's even more of a better place to be in, be single, heal, recover and don't beat yourself up for the wrong, but allow yourself to process your experience before connecting yourself into another relationship.

A good friend of mine named Victor married young like I did and to the public eye he had it all but in him he knew that he was nowhere near the man that everyone was praising him to be. I remember talking with him one evening and he started sharing with me some heart wrenching things that blew my mind, how he had married his wife and would keep

her pregnant so he could go spend time with his other women. There was nothing in my natural understanding that was able to understand his methodology to dealing with his marriage.
His wife really had no idea for what she was in for. Pregnant now with his 4th child and just recently suffering a miscarriage, Victor kept doing his thing in the streets with his women. While standing there talking with him I was trying to figure out how this story would play out and end but I stopped and let him finish his own story.

While Victor was out in the street with his women, his wife was home nursing his young children and caring for the soon to be new edition. Victor comes home from work one day, not going over to his other woman's house, but for the first time in 5 years came straight home from work to his family. Staggering into the door after drinking on the walk home, looks his wife in the eyes, drunk with the smell of vodka on his breath, his wife Emily rubbing her pregnant stomach looking his face with concern waiting for what he would say next.

"Honey, I don't deserve you". Emily's eyes watered, she ran over to him pulling him by the arm, "what do you mean???" Victor so drunk he decides to let the truth out about how he's spent the first years of their marriage up to the present moment. "Emily, I am a no good man, cheater… OK… I am no good… I don't deserve you"… His wife had no idea the truth would one day come down on her like this. Pulling her hair she started screaming, "No… No… No…" all the while beating Victor on his chest, Victor made the decision he could live with whatever her answer would be at that moment. They tried working their marriage out as he informed me but a year and a half later still ended up in divorce.

Victor was telling me his problem was from a young man he watch his father come home to his mother, but he knew his father always had other women; some even lived in the community where he grew up. I remember him telling me a mutual friend of ours was really his brother from one of his father's women. At that moment my mind was shattered, thinking I was the only one going through a hard time, rough family and not knowing what to do. Victor said he turned to women thinking he could wash off his hatred for his father and the pain he suffered from his childhood. In that same moment I also learned that victor had grew up getting molested by one of his step brothers.

Victor thought the more he slept with women it would take away the pain of what he had experienced in his crippling preteens. The nights that he fought off his father's child from another woman, stripping him of his manhood in the night. My mouth rattled like an elderly person trying to fix their dentures in their mouth, I could not believe what I had learned. Victor told me how he knew he was wrong for what he did to his wife. Their marriage ended in divorce.

While Victor had a painful past that drove him to the streets, I want any man reading this book to understand no matter what you habit or problem is, it's not an excuse to misuse or mistreat a woman. Be man enough to come clean, admit your faults and work on them if you can.

## Now let's talk about the 5 stages of recovery:

### Stage One: Denial

During the denial phase, you may try to convince yourself that your marriage is not really over, that somehow everything will work out. Or, your denial may be denying that you even feel any grief. If you find yourself saying to people early on in your divorce that you are over it, then you may be setting yourself up for depression. The truth of the matter when I experienced the betrayal of an unfaithful wife I was ready to end and walk away from my marriage because I knew if I didn't it would turn me into a bitter man.

The dangerous thing about denial is most of the time all the warning signs are present to let you know that you're happy home is deteriorating. Yet you may be so engulfed in love that you really don't see the reality of what's before you. Friends and family can warn you and tell you but somehow you just don't see it until you are ready to perceive it.

## **Stage Two: Anger**

The next stage is the anger. There may be a number of factors helping to fuel this. Some things may involve Infidelity, abandonment, being left with the responsibility of the home and or the children or feeling like you have been cut out of your family's lives. These among other things can all work together to fuel that anger. Who wrote the book that says men don't become angry and bitter? Truth is a man is capable of experiencing any emotion that a woman can feel we just play them out differently.

When the anger starts to fade, often people find themselves bargaining with their ex husband or wife as if by settling something, the pain will go away. This happens even when couples split and have not maintain the lines of communication. Somehow the door reopens and after the anger has subside your looking to mend and fix all the wrongs and put back together the relationship you once had. This doesn't always work out well for everyone. So what begins to happen with some people is that they will go through cycles of bitterness and anger. It's like an emotional roller coaster. One minute you feel OK and you can take on the world, ready to get back out their find a new love and start dating again. Then in next day has a whole new set of feelings that you dread because they slowly creep up on your and paralyze you from moving forward in life.

## Stage Three: Bargaining

One of the stages of recovery from a bad divorce is bargaining. After you get over the anger, the hurt, devastation and the betrayal, or whatever your set of problems maybe that cause a close to come to you bliss, once the dust settles you start thinking of ways to try to make it work. You start telling yourself ill just pretend it didn't happen or that I am happy when you know you are opening yourself up for a sour chance in hell that those things would ever successfully happen.

The bargaining stage is a dangerous place to be in and often times go hand and hand with denial. Not wanting to accept that it's already over or trying to bring the dead relationship back to life again. If the truth be told you're better off being stable by yourself and allowing yourself to heal then to reopen the wound of that relationship trying to rekindle it or bargain you way through it.

## Stage Four: Depression

Depression is that feeling of deep sadness and is more than likely still mixed with a little anger. Depression is that numbness that you feel, the daze that you're in but don't know symptomatically when you arrived there, you just know that one day you're lost your grip. At this stage your severely affected often seek help before finally settling into the acceptance stage. But by the time you finally reach a healthy acceptance, it is time to pick up the pieces and rebuild your new life.

See, the problem with this stage is not every man responds' the same way. Some men go into deep modes of depression not taking care of him-self as he would normally do; his appearance, dress and hygiene. Others go into venerability dating, finding a replacement and rapping their lives around that person, often not fully committing just using them to get over. No matter how you look at it the depression stage of the game is no place to be. Anyone that's in this place often doesn't know it until they are well into it.

## Stage Five: Acceptance

The best part of the process is when you have gone through stage one through four and arrive to stage five. You can put you bags down, rest a while but the battle is not over yet. The reason I said put your bags down is because everyone comes out of a relationship still carrying things from the previous. Just take a minute to rest, breathe and recover from the blows, mentally, emotionally, and sometimes physically that you have had to endure.

Acceptance is the biggest part of the deal and it gets harder when you admit who was at fault for the break up. Maybe you were in adultery and it's your fault factually as to why your marriage ended, maybe you grew apart over time, or could it be a money matter that brought on the strain? Truly it doesn't matter the right or the wrong, it's a broken relationship, your human, and deserve to be healed.

Acceptance and assessing the damage no matter where you are with it is the hard part. Even if the fault was not yours at all, you still have a fault in it. No one's perfect, yet sometimes we don't always do everything that we should do to save our marriages and be the person for the role we take on.
When you accept that it's over, that's the major road opening to your healing, after that your well on your way to a full recovery. Accept that it's over, move on mentally and emotionally. Detach yourself from things that remind you about the marriage, the pain, the regret, everyday becomes easier than the day before and long before your know it you will be skipping, dancing, singing again and ready to live life again.

# Diary Of An Ex-Husband

# Chapter Three:

## The Big Announcement

*"If I love you have lost its meaning, where do you now stand?" Michael McCain*

Eric Jones walks in the door to his New Jersey condo, after a long day of work. Walks over to his wife standing in the kitchen, hugs kisses and greets her as he would usually do and Stacey looks her loving husband in the eyes and say's "honey how was your day?", Eric loosens his tie and heads for the refrigerator for something refreshing to drink, pours his drink as he responds to his wife, "stressful but, hey… I made it". Stacey then responds and says, "Well that's good honey, glad you made it through". Eric smiles, looks his wife in the face and says, "I can tell you have something more you want to say so what is it?" Stacy is twirling her fingers with a rubber band from cutting up the broccoli for

## Diary Of An Ex-Husband

dinner. Stacy responds, "Honey you already expressed you had a stressful day so I really don't want to add to that right now". Eric assures his wife that no matter what his personal stresses are there's always opportunity to talk.

Stacey starts sweating, belts out "I want a divorce". Under the shock of his wife's statement, Eric drops his glass of orange juice, "you want a what?" glass now everywhere, "A divorce Eric"... Stacy bellows out with a sigh. The problem with this marriage was that Stacy had threaten a divorce so many times before, even went to counseling, tried taking a break from the marriage and at one point started seeing a co-worker on her job. Much of this went on for years all while Eric spent long hours of hard work on his job as a lawyer for a major New York law firm.

Eric with tears in his eyes gripping his head yells with deepness in his voice that thundered, "What did I do wrong?" While Eric stood waiting for answers, his wife proceeded to pull the divorce papers out her purse and slide them across the counter. Eric almost drunk in his shock, just says, "You're going to end it like this?" Stacey never answered; Eric signed the papers, while tears co-signed his signature.

The point here is, there's no greater emotional pain that can be inflicted upon a man that the announcement by his wife that she wants a divorce. Eric must have felt like he was repeatedly being stabbed in his heart, but somehow finding the strength not to respond in anger, signed the papers and decided to let go of a 15 year marriage, 4 kids, condo, staggered into his BMW and drove back to his office and spent the night there.

The truth is in the divorce process even if both parties have "seen it coming" for some time, the announcement really comes as no big surprise, the actual announcement goes off like a bomb in your face that's been ticking all this time and finally the big boom came.

# I think I am sick

Eric Jones staggered back into his New York office to sit at his desk to try to configure a plan as to how he would pick his life back up from the place he just drove up into like a freak accident. His whole world came crashing down on him and the flood of emotions Eric was feeling made it no better. Eric tossed his family photos into his trash can by his desk, but held the photos for a moment, thinking about his vows.

To honor...

To obey...

To be supportive of..

To stand beside in good times and bad...

Through sickness and health...

For richer or poorer, now no longer wanting your love.

## Diary Of An Ex-Husband

Eric Just took the hardest blow to a man's emotional equilibrium, just about the most damaging illness you can ever face in your lifetime. The heart break of a marriage you sacrifice your all for is now ending like it never started. It's not until you have been smacked with such pain that you soon have to face the reality that after you walk away from this life goes on, you will recover. I can admit that when you're going through it, it really does feel like the end of the world and times won't get any better from here. Take it from someone who had to walk away just like Eric; I too had to one day made my announcement.

The bright side of things from here is now you have the time to realign your life and find your peace and true happiness again. Truth of the matter is when you're married you live so much for the person your conjoined to that you sacrifice who you truly are to become one with someone who doesn't always agree on your goals, visions and aspirations. Yes it hurts but this is a fine opportunity to get back on the road to being you all over again. Take this time to know that this is a chapter that's turning in your life but the story really doesn't end here.

Every breakup and divorce is different, but there's one thing you must do if you want keep your sanity. Quickly sever all ties with that person, clean up all the odds and ends while it's in your power to do it. If feasible move into a new home, relocate so the memory of where you once lived with this spouse doesn't have to haunt you. If you must stay where you're at, redecorate and change the look or feel of the place. Get rid of things that remind you of them. Change your number. Once a woman makes an announcement she no longer wants you for a husband you one have two options, counseling and going for a walk that you just don't come back from.

From the moment a woman makes the announcement that she wants a divorce it's time to start thinking about your survival and your mental health. As peacefully as you can gather your life together and prepare to move on. Arguing and fighting will not be worth it, it will only make you surer that you want to end the marriage. A bitter, hurt, scorned, or undesirable wife may say something's in her pain that will eat away at you like cancer if you don't deal with this with the right mindset. After all you knew by this point you marriage was on the rocks, you just didn't think it would all go down the way it just did.

As devastating as the moment was for Eric, he eventually had to pick his life up from his ruins and face the music again. It's funny how you can be in something one day and your whole life change the next. It's amazing how people can say "I do" and then turn into the bride from hell or in some cases a husband from hell. No matter the case, Eric's life will be very different from here on. Sometimes fighting for a person who doesn't want to love you is an already fix fight. Blow after blow trying to remedy the situation to love on someone who keeps growing apart from you on a daily basis.

Just like Eric I know what it's like to be in a marriage to someone and move on but you're still in it. The thing people didn't know about Eric was he learned to live with his pain, he learned to live with the fact that his wife used his long hours at work to her advantage to go see other men. It didn't really matter if Eric worked long nights or came home; the truth was Stacey had already made up in her mind and heart she was going to do her thing anyway.

# Lord, rebuild me

Losing a wife or marriage is just like losing a vital organ of your body. You will suffer some pain; you will need some time to recover. You might not be able to return to life as usual, it's OK to take a few days to recover, just don't let it be a long time. You must let go of that chapter of your life and the sooner you let go and completely end it, the sooner you will be able to start rebuilding your life and ultimately find the happiness you want and desire. Between the time your wife announces the end of your marriage, or maybe it's you that took the deciding into your own hands. When you face it, you're going to hurt like you never imagined.
You're going to go through a number of mental and emotional changes and phases. One thing you will start to take note of is the process is necessary to "heal yourself".

Even though it hurts you have to let go, you'll never be able to enjoy life or love again if you don't. True happiness will start to fade quickly if you wallow in the pain of what you just experienced. While I can admit that most men recover 10xs faster from relationship break ups, all men are not the same. Some men are not mentally equipped to bring themselves to terms to deal with the battles they face after. You have to discharge the past from your system and grasp your happiness as if it were a fleeting garment in the wind.

Think of your divorce like a man going for a bike ride who hits a bump falls and scrapes his knee on the pavement. It's going to hurt, it's going to bleed and even scab, but with the proper care and time, you will recover. Sadly divorces are common and you're not the only person going through one. Oddly enough you might even know someone else going through one who seems to be handling it different from you.

Most people going through a divorce want to deny that it's happening at first; you may pretend that it's a bad dream or a nightmare. Some even look at it like it's a joke until the reality of things settle with them. Believe it or not this type of thinking is normal, but it prolongs the agony of your hurt when you won't face your reality head on. Many people try not to think about it or face it, making yourself busy not to deal with the matter at hand is not going to help either, the quicker it's over the better you will feel. Accept that the marriage is over and then start your road to new beginnings.

In spite of the emotional and mental anguish you need to find a personal meditation and decree that's going to help pull you through this experience. For every person it's different, some might turn to scriptures for comfort, others might turn to prayer and meditation. What I would like to suggest is power affirmations that will help settle your spirit and something to suggest to your mind to think on instead of the pain.

My personal affirmation was also a prayer that I personally asked God to help me with and that was "Lord, rebuild me". No matter if you're ready for the divorce or not, it's still a broken relationship, its still brokenness you experience, weather ready or not.

## Chapter Four:

## Trick or Treat

*True Love waits, Lust wants instant gratification. Michael McCain-*

Just like the windy days of autumn the leaves on the trees are turning their best colors for fall Jason Armbrister was feeling the heart throbs of preparing to pop the big question to his girlfriend of one year. There was an excitement stirring up on the inside he could barely hide. So he calls his girlfriend, tells her to prepare for a date out to dinner and to put on her best outfit while he went to pick up the rings he would propose with. Jason hides the ring inside his Italian leather jacket. They arrive to a Bronx BBQ's on Fordham Rd. ordered their dinner sat and laughed and talked as they would usually do, and then he pulled out the box and asked Alera Rivera his girlfriend of 1 year to marry him.

# Diary Of An Ex-Husband

Jason Armbrister had no clue what he was headed for, he felt he was deeply in love and nothing could change his mind. Yet his sweetheart Alera was harboring secrets and habits in a Pandora's Box that would one day crush Jason's life. Jason and Alera married in 2004 at city hall in New York. While Jason was full of the joy of now having a wife and preparing to be the man of the house and taking on his new family and responsibility. His now wife Alera was harboring some deep secrets.

Alera since the age of 15 years old had been exploring her sexuality, not knowing that 2 years later she would pay for it at the age of 17 getting pregnant and found that it was too late to get an abortion. Alera thought that the abortion would be her way out but after her doctor's visit found out that she was too far along to consider that at that moment. So she had to return home from boot camp to break the news to her Aunt Lora who was her adoptive mother she called "mom".

Alera was not only a promiscuous young lady but she came from a ruff family. Alera's mom was a drug addict who was even a user during her pregnancy with Alera. Which needless to say she was born a crack baby, her father died when she was 6 months old really leaving her with no real support and care. So she went up for adoption and her Aunt Lora, "mom" came to get her. Lora raised her to the best of her abilities but there was just something in Alera that seemed to be generational. It was as if the streets were calling her and she could not resist it. Alera would get into fight after fight, try skipping school and her grades were being affected by it so "mom" put her into boot camp hoping that it would discipline her and she would shape up into a better young lady.

Here it is, Alera returns home from boot camp, she was put out because her counselors found out that she was pregnant. So now it was time to break the news to mom and her knowing her mom would be furious because trouble is what brought her to the boot camp in the first place, now a baby on top of trouble didn't seem to make the picture any better than what it presently was.

Lora walks through the halls of the boot camp greeting and saying hello to the other young girls who was there, arrives to the main office and asked to speak to Mrs. Banks. Another secretary directed her to Mrs. Banks office and when entering the room she looked at Alera with a silence that was so cold, greeted Mrs. Banks and took her seat. She knew being called back to the boot camp was no good news. So Mrs. Banks gets out of her seat, walks across the room and greets Mrs. Lora Rivera, I am Mrs. Banks. After the greeting Mrs. Banks returned to her seat and says, I know you may not know why you're here today, but I want you to know that I love Alera allot and she's grown on me in the short time she's been here but I want to inform you that we have a problem.

Mrs. Rivera squirms in her seat, her mellow yellow skin now turning beat red as she prepares for the news Mrs. Banks had to give her. Well... Mrs. Rivera, we recently sent all the young ladies in our boot camp for checkups with our campus medical team as you know that's a part of our policies here. It's been one week since after finding out that your

lovely daughter Alera is 3 months pregnant. What!?!?! ... Echoed out of Mrs. Rivera's mouth; as she looks across the room at Alera.
Yes, that's what the problem is and as much as we would like to help you Mrs. Rivera and your daughter Alera we cannot keep her here. Mrs. Banks took a sigh and waited for her reply. Mrs. Rivera with tears in her eyes says; I understand… so what's the discharge process is? Mrs. Banks said she could sign the papers and return to pick up Alera next Monday. Mrs. Rivera wiping tears out her eyes, walked out the office without even speaking to her daughter and said I'll see you on Monday Mrs. Banks.

# 7 Months later

Alera's home now, her adoptive sister and brother are happy she's back, shocked she's pregnant. Even though Lora was not happy she took all measures on preparing to be a grandmother and fix a room for her daughter and the new born. Alera came home from St. Barnabas Hospital giving birth to a healthy baby boy! The excitement was high, people seemed to pay more attention to the baby then they did Alera. The other problem was from day one, no one knew who or where his father was. Alera refused to talk about it, she attempt to contact the family herself and no avail. The boy's mother told her that was not his child and to say out of their life, so that exactly what Alera did, heartbroken and all she learned how to take care of her own son with very little help from anyone but "mom".

Alera turned to the welfare system as most single non-working mothers did in the Bronx. Yet it didn't seem to be enough to make ends meet. Lora was growing tired while with a crying baby at night and an extra mouth to feed. So after one year she asked Alera to go into the shelter and get her own place, she felt she was entitled to it and it would be best for her to be on her own. Alera was more stressed than ever, failing the G.E.D. test every time she took it now under the pressure of being put out. So she left, and went to live with another aunt and her baby boy Emory was just over a year now. Alera was determined to make life better for her and her son, so she signed up to attend Monroe College taking classes in business administration while trying to earn her associates and G.E.D. 2 years later meeting her soon to be husband Jason Armbrister.

# Her-Story

We have all heard of history, but this now is her-story, the story behind the history of this young lady. All while Alera was fighting to make it in the wild streets of the Bronx. Now a high school dropout and trying to raise a son, Alera had some habits that she tried to keep bottled up. Alera was very promiscuous and had a sex addiction. Alera was a very attractive young lady but had very poor self-esteem. She dated and played the harlot with some of the most unattractive men. She only used them for whatever her personal reasons were. She had men she would date that she turned to just to have sex and some were for sex but kind of like friends with benefits. If she gave you some, you had to give her something she needed in return, which was usually money or things she needed for her son. As disheartening as this truth is this was the life Alera lived.

While Jason is just now coming into the picture he could see something's but never thought that it was as bad as what they were. Jason thought how bad can this girl really be? Jason thought it would be worth it to build a family with her. Coming into an already made family with a step son was not half bad considering he was used to caring for other peoples kids and had grew up too fast himself. Jason met Alera in church, which was another reason he felt that she was a young lady trying to get her life together and was in the right place if that's what she was trying to do.

What Jason didn't know was there were several men within that church that his wife had been sleeping with. Some were the preacher's kids, the sons of the elders of the church, some of the younger deacons who were in their 30's and one or two regular members of the church. Not to mention some men she met at work or that attended Monroe College with her. As crazy as it may sound this was the hidden life Alera lived, the heart break that Jason was in for would send his life spiraling out of control.

Alera tried hiding most of her life style from her husband as best as she could, she pretended to go spend the weekend with her girlfriends while she would go out for a few hours to see her men, have sex and return to her friend's house to act as if she had been there the whole time. Jason and his wife was young and he knew trying to stay home every weekend would not work, he didn't want to keep his wife from enjoying life just because they were married but never imagined what was going on behind his back.

# The Dream

One day, Jason wakes up with night sweats and shakes his wife to tell her about a dream he had. He was describing what he thought to be a dream but was really a message from God unfolding revealing his wife's secret life. While it was not in Jason's mind to accuse his wife of anything he knew exactly what the dream meant, because he knew he had the gift to dream and receive messages. So he started sharing the dream with his wife and told her what he saw and how he saw a man approaching her, asking her to go out with him and even boldly asking if he could have sex with her.

In the dream Jason saw his wife in rare form, the person he didn't know he was married to. Yet he had no proof other than the dream that this is what was happening. He continued telling her the dream he told her the guy was a heavy set bus driver who drove the Bronx 17 bus, and he was about 37 years old and light skin and his name was Kevin. His wife jumped up and said she would be right back, running into the bathroom with her cell phone telling her girlfriend that her husband somehow knew everything that was going on. Her girlfriend Lydia on the other end of the phone was trying to tell her to calm down and was trying to make sense of what she was talking about.

Jason knocked on the bathroom door repeatedly as he had heard her whispering on the phone. It was not until that moment that it all sunk in, all of his premonitions on his wife before marrying her was right. Jason had several conversations with his wife about things he saw and wanted to deal with before getting married, yet his wife assured him that she was OK and was ready to be married. Jason knew from over hearing the conversation in the bathroom he was ready to end and walk away from it all. He asked his wife to attend some counseling, she said no. He asked his wife to try to take some time to purge out of her life any connection, friend, **ex-**boyfriend or man who had an interest in her that she knew would be a hindrance to their marriage. She agrees on that, and promised her husband that she would do as he requested. Jason in his free time called his best friend to tell him what he just learned, his friend knowing from the beginning all of the things Jason had a problem with was just as shocked as his friend was. He encouraged him to stick it out and try to make it work so that was now Jason's plan.

Jason gave his wife six months to try to work on some of the things that were going wrong with their marriage; he stared laying down the law in other words. They had many discussions about how to be married, married life, what was OK and not OK. He encouraged his wife that in spite of them both coming from imperfect families that their future was in their own reach and they had a chance at making the life for themselves that they wanted. He told his wife the business he started was all for her and his step son to make sure he had a way to provide for his family. Yet to Alera she could not break free from her habits, no amount of sexual intimacy with her husband seemed to change her, no gifts he could buy, no trips they could go on could change anything. Alera was dealing with the seed of something that has now grown roots in her life sucking the life out of everything positive that's trying to grow in her life.

# Dirty Laundry

Jason worked hard; he owned a cleaning business and had landed a big contract with a millionaire preacher in New York making around 5,000 a month. He sent for his best friend to move to New York to partner with his business and they started making money. Soon, weekends were not needed; Alera started waiting till her husband went to work to go do her thing with her men, just making sure that she got home before he did. To everyone else they had the perfect marriage to be a young newlywed couple just 2 years now into their marriage. They attended church regularly and many people looked up to them and respected them. Going into their third year of marriage Jason made up his mind that he could not take it anymore, he was ready to walk away from his marriage as the evidence of what his wife was doing was piling up but again, he had no way to prove it but he was following his intuition and his gut.

Alera tried the reverse psychology thing accusing her husband of cheating on her and seeing other people when he would be out at work or at church. Many nights he was pulling over nights at work with his cleaning business. Soon those over nights became a regular habit and way of life for him to deal with a wife he no longer wanted to come home to. He tried over and over again gaining and understanding form his wife on what was going on in her life. They talked about her families past and things she had gone through, he wanted her to see that some habits she had formed were un-healthy for their marriage never demanding change but giving her the space to pick up that change for herself.

Soon Jason grew tired of being the father and not the husband. That's what Jason described the experience to be like. Married to a woman who is not yet whole enough to mature and do what a woman is required to do. Jason saw how trying to work it out by advice from some of his mentors was not working either. Soon they parted ways for a few months and it was the first break up and separation they had in 3 years since they had been married. Jason though it was a good experience because his wife came back to him asking for his forgiveness and help. Jason thought it was the perfect opportunity to work things out and learned that that was nowhere near was about to happen.

Jason welcomed his wife back into his home and tried to start dating and building their relationship up again from the ruins that it was in. Alera had not changed one bit, Alera had a so called best friend that she had messed around with off and on who she was starting to sleep with again named Jermaine. Jason not having a clue continued doing what he felt was best to help fix the marriage and win his wife back all the while Alera should have won an academy award for the way she led her husband on, she did whatever he asked, looked him in the face every day and told him "I love you Jason".

Jason had prepared a romantic night with his wife and purchases some bottles of wine, ran a nice tub of water with rose petals in it, with candles all around the bed room and the bathroom. He was preparing for a romantic night and celebrating their reunion and wanted it to be special. Just when you think things can't get any worse than what they have been Jason was hit with blow to his emotional equilibrium that would almost destroy him.

Jason and his wife sat in the tub washed each other up, kissed and cuddled playing with the soap suds and rose petals. Tipsy from the wine and both agreeing it was time to get out of the tub they staggered into the room laughing and echoing whispers suggestive of the sparks that was about to fly off in their bed room. Jason laying in the bed with Alera and soon rolling around while they were kissing, he got on top of his wife and penetrated her. After a few strokes while she proceeded to moan and grip his back he began to sense something was wrong. His wife continued moaning and pulling him so close you would think they were one, he started thinking about the difference he felt in his wife's vagina.

## Diary Of An Ex-Husband

It was loose! Jason felt his heart panting twice the amount of times that it usually would from the activity they were practicing and he looked into his wife's eyes, without her having a clue as to what was on his mind, he said, "I thought you told me you loved me?" She looked him in his eyes gripping him and attempting to kiss him, "I do"... Jason pulled himself off of her and she was left looking confused. He went into the shower and began washing himself scrubbing his skin until it felt sore.

Jason knew at that moment his wife had been sleeping with someone else and knew that this man's penis was significantly larger than his since he had the ability to notice the room in her vagina. While Jason knew he was no sex expert, he had been around the block a few times and noticed one of the things his wife would do before engaging in sex was douche. It was not only a way of cleaning her private area but an age old trick some women used to tightening up their vaginal walls. At that moment Jason walked out of his house and went to visit his cousin in Riverdale, sat with her and told her a few things about his marriage he had kept from everyone else.

Alera was still confused at what happened and brought their night of passion short. While Jason was at his cousins house, what do you think Alera went to do, she went to go visit Jermaine who happened to live not too far way. Jason came back home to an empty house the next day and a few hours later she came in the door with her bags and things form the night before and the arguing began. For as sensitive of the situation to be, she never owned up to cheating on her husband but continued to accuse him of cheating on her and seeing other people. She voiced how she did not believe he was working or at church some of the nights he went out, she even went as far as saying she had proof he was cheating because people told her some things. Jason looked his wife in the eyes for as calm of a manner he could muster and asked his wife to tell him the truth. She kept assuring him she was innocent. He brought up the loose vagina experience from the night before that still had his mind going in circles, she had the nerve to look shocked but quickly fixed her facial expressions again telling him he was crazy and no such thing happened. Later that night she text Lydia again and told her how she had messed up and Jason found out because she was loose. When Alera went to sleep she knew he could find evidence on her phone so he forwarded all her text messages from Jermaine and Lydia to his phone and saved them it was the first confirming evidence that he knew what he knew and was right this whole time.

# Broken Revenge

Jason still taking his late hours at work, working with his best friend then made a whole life change. He stared making new friends, hanging out with people sometimes in unlikely places that he would normally not be in. Soon dating other women and his self-esteem had been deeply affected. He began doing as his wife had done cheating. He went out on numerous innocent dates, just trying to emotionally purge what he had been through by trying to enjoy life again and muster up the strength to either fix or end his marriage. Soon two of the women he started seeing wanted more than just a date and nice night out on the town. While this whole time he had never had sex outside his marriage that was about to quickly end. Jason felt like he should get back at his wife for what she put him through.

Patrice loved Jason, was hoping that she could even win his heart from his wife and they would soon be together. Jason at some point came to Patrice after 3 months of seeing each other and asked to bring an end to what they had been doing. Jason was growing bitter and angry; he knew he could never be the type of person his wife had been to him this whole time so he decided stop and take the time he needed to gather himself together from a broken place that he was in. He soon separated himself from many of his friends and stopped seeing some friends he made. Patrice was his only relationship out of his marriage and he had many other offers but never took up the opportunity.

Jason was surrounded by women who would tell him his wife didn't know what to do with him, as if to suggest that they knew and that they knew how to please him and make his life better. While in an already bad situation there was something about Jason different that you just couldn't shake his love for his wife. He knew he was not perfect had recently done things he was not proud of so he made the decision to end his marriage and walk way. He remained single and by himself. When he decided to end his marriage his wife accused him of having someone that he was with, which was not true, Jason from months ago ended his fling and settled his life.

## Diary Of An Ex-Husband

Now it was time to end this bad marriage which he began to feel like it was turning him into a man that he was not. He started hating his wife, the love he once had for her was now completely gone. To the public eye, he and his wife up held each other with so much respect. People had no idea what was going on in their marriage unless they decided to let you in on what happen. Alera started telling Jason's closes friends, he was a cheater and had done all these things to her while they were married, he beat her, was abusive to his step son which none of those thing were true at all. She knew that her marriage was headed for an end and wanted people to be on her side so she did whatever she could to get people on her side. Guess what? It worked for a while; people fell for the bait, all because people wanted to know a thing or two about Jason's personal life and wanted all the juicy gossip they could get.

Jason beat his self-up for the wrong he did do at that end by seeing other women, but that guilt was short lived when the reality of what he lived with now for four years was before him. During this time Jason learned all about some of his wife's flings and habits probably in more detail then what he wanted to hear. She had begun telling some of his closest friends about how she slept with members of his church, how she had abortions and she even started sharing this information with other religious leaders that Jason was close with. They all turned on him; because she was telling stories about things she said he did which were not true. Even though he's not perfect the lies she was telling were definitely not the truth. It's funny how she could make up stories about him but not tell the dirt that she had been doing this whole time.

Soon, she didn't need to tell it, it came out. People started learning about what she was doing, seeing Alera in places with men and doing things that they knew was not right. People didn't know how to break the news to Jason so they stayed out of it hoping that Jason would find out on his own. With all of this going on there's no need to tell you that people in and out of the church were gossiping and talking. Jason had already separated from his wife she was living in a shelter and to make matters worse she was pregnant, he was taking the heat from people over it because no one understood why he had put her out. The problem was all the mess came out about her sleeping around, which then turned Jason to the streets himself. Pulling himself back up out of it he decided to walk away from it all baby or not.

## Chapter Five:

## Every Man Has A Breaking Point

*You can spend your life being strong for others but there comes a time when you have to be strong for yourself.*

*Michael McCain-*

One thing that I've learned in the process of my go though is that I am no supper human, every man has a breaking point. I don't care how nice and how loving or forgiving you are, no amount of prayer or meditation will keep a man from responding in anger or bitterness when the mess just keeps on coming and there seems to be no end. Can I just be real with you? Most men hide their real pain only reveling it to those they choose to. Men hurt just like women do and sometimes that pain will lead you down avenues you don't want to visit. The worst thing you can do is fall into sex traps, emotional surrogates because your present marriage is not working. But guess what? It doesn't stop people from doing it.

I can tell you that in my marriage I held on for dear life, yes I saw plenty of signs that it was winding down to an end but I wasn't about to let that happen without a fight. So I fought back as best that I could and still didn't win, and today I can stand here and tell you that loosing that fight was probably the best fight I've ever lost in life. For another man, your story may be different, you story maybe that fighting for your family or marriage was the best thing you've done because in the end you won the battle, but sometime you have to understand that all wars are not created equal. Someone walks away a winner and another walks away a looser. Sometimes being the looser is the best life lesson you can come out with because it builds your momentum to come out on top of life and declare yourself a winner.

# Confronting a Cheating Spouse

Living under the suspicion of a cheating spouse will drive you crazy. I know plenty of people who say they have "intuition" on situations with their spouse and somewhere right and others were so far from the truth that it was downright embarrassing. Before I give you my tips on confronting your cheating spouse also allow me to say this, when you're in a relationship and you have what they call "a feeling" or "intuition" that your spouse is cheating; be prepared when you go probing for the evidence. I've seen countless people who out of anger, hurt or raw emotion start responding to "the feeling" but no ready to face the truth they may uncover. Finding the truth that your spouse is cheating is only one part of it, if you go looking for proof you will find it. If you go probing for information you will always come up with what you're looking for.

Sometimes you may discover you have a flirtatious spouse, can you handle the truth you're standing in? Can you face the facts and the evidence that you will find? Here is where I would like to offer some tips on confronting a cheating spouse and these tips are actual steps I walked out in my own personal marriage myself.

## **Step One**: Seek a professional relationship counselor:

While I would like to recommend people to pray or meditate to relive the stress that they may be feeling the truth of the matter is, no matter how much you pray when you're dealing with this type of pressure, when your confronting something a prayer will be far from what's on your lips. Not every couple has the privilege of talking things out like sensible adults. So seek a professional counselor that you may confide your story in, any suspicions you have about your marriage and see what advice they have to offer you.

While talking with your counselor you should be able to come up with sound tactics for approaching you spouse without it turning into an all-out brawl. Which is using wisdom on your part, I don't recommend talking it over with friends and family because if your marriage is still salvageable they will always hold anger or them being to privy to your business they will always hold it against your spouse and you may have moved on and remedied the problem in your marriage. Your best bet is to find a relationship counselor that can walk you through some advice and a plan you're your marriage.

**Step Two:** Talk To Your Spouse About Your Suspicions:

While I can admit this is not an easy step and some people think they are ready to just step head on into it my advice would be to remain calm, be reasonable and be rational. The truth be told if your spouse really is cheating on you they are already prepared to be presented with allegations about what they are doing. So your tactic here is not to bring up the issue in an offensive manner, this will only make your spouse respond in a defensive frame of mind.

As crazy as it may sound you want your spouse to be comfortable and at easy with any information they are giving you. Your spouse is more likely to tell the truth if they feel like you are not going to go crazy on them for what they are doing.

Remember to remain calm as possible, try not to display that you are upset or emotional. Your spouse will try to play on your anger or your sympathy, right now what you're aiming for is the truth. So be calm as a cucumber and roll with the punches. It's important to play it cool if you want to try to save your marriage. It's also important if you intend to divorce your spouse. Once you obtain the information you are aiming for whatever choice you make after is completely up to you.

If you keep a common sense and rational outlook while getting this information out of your spouse the chances are you're going to get the truth in its full scope. The information you're presented with is what you will have left to decide how life goes on from that point. The person who usually acts more sensible in times like these usually controls the outcome of the situation anyway. Arguing and a done me wrong song is not what you want this information for. You wanted this information to bring your mental torment to an end and receive answers to your suspicions that you have been carrying around.

## Step Three: Hire An Expert:

If you feel that you cannot trust your spouse to be honest enough to tell the truth about their affairs then hire a professional. This may be best if you feel that you can't handle confronting your spouse in asking yourself or to avoid confrontation with them. If you feel that your spouse is in an affair then it is time to let someone who is trained to confirm your suspicions. The worst thing you can do is try to investigate yourself. Don't follow your spouse around, that will only make things worse, if you're caught it will lead to a confrontation you may not be ready for and that's not healthy for no one who's involved.

Trying to investigate on a cheating spouse on your own sometimes will lead you to trip and flip over things which might not even be evidence. Another truth about trying to plot your own investigation is that if you sit around prying for information you will find something great or small but will you be ready for what you find? Your best bet is to hire a private investigator that can confirm to you your suspicions and leave them at rest with evidence.

Should you decide to aim for a divorce after that you will have evidence from a private investigator which can be used in divorce court. Any information found on your spouse is admissible without prejudice and in the end it will be worth every penny you paid for it.

## **Step Four:** Consult A Divorce Attorney:

After confirming your spouse is cheating and you decide to divorce, consult with an attorney. Be very careful taking advice from friends and family members at this point on what method to go about a divorce, it will only confuse you. You should never be discussion your problems with people who don't have the advice or the power to solve them, so stick to the professionals who will be able to give sound advice and legal advice.

Your attorney will give you legal advice on what your options are, your state's laws pertaining to infidelity and what your next move should be. Most states have what they call a "no-fault divorce" some are free and others you may have to pay for. The judge still has discretion when deciding divorce cases so, be mindful of this, the more causable evidence you have in your favor the better. Some states even have laws that if you and your spouse have been separated for over 6 months to a year and it's a broken marriage they may grant you the divorce even with no evidence.

While you are going under divorce proceedings your best bet is to stay clear of your spouse and any person they maybe in an affair with. You do not want any conflict to come up during your court proceedings on arrest, assault charges or otherwise that can likely happen from trying to confront the situation on your own. Your best bet is to follow your attorney's advice, after all that's what you hired them for in the first place.

## **Step Five:** Talk to the right people:

I can't begin to stress to you enough how important it is for anyone who is going through a divorce to keep your private life just that, PRIVATE! Your family members only need to know the basics. If you have children you should never ever discuss you cheating spouse with them. No matter how old your children maybe they do not need to hear your breakdown of the story. A professional family counselor can give you some tips and advice on a method to breaking the news to your children without all the gory details.

Your family and friends need not be privy to everything as well; they will never let you live it down. One day you might want to marry again and not relive the story of how the last relationship did not work and why. It would be fully up to you if you share that information with a new spouse or someone you are dating. Sometimes your family and friends think they are helping you think on a level plain but in reality they are butting in areas that you may not be asking for their help in.

Taking time to talk with a support counselor or professional will allow you the opportunity to get out any anger or bitterness you may be feeling from what you just experienced. Another good way of purging out some of these feelings would be to write about it or make a video to yourself describing all the things that's on your mind, how you are feeling, what's the plan for how you will pick up your life from where you are. You can share that with your support counselor or relationship counselor and they can help walk you through your healing process.

## **Step Six:** Surround Yourself With a Positive Support System:

No matter how prepared you were to discover your spouse was unfaithful, you might be able to live with the suspicion but when you have the truth or evidence before you it's an emotional blow that can lead to a break down. I say it all the time, who says that men don't cry? While some men may not cry, they become enraged and angered over what they have just experienced feeling played and reacts to that feeling. It becomes unhealthy not only to you who are going through it but to others you are in relationship with.

While I am not big on telling your business to family and friends, you will need a network of supporters to hold you up during this time of what you are going through. Just because a person is there to support you does not mean you have to be telling all your gut wrenching details about your life and marriage. Sometimes it's best to just allow them to be an emotional support, a friend, a family member who you can enjoy life around without separating all your dirty laundry with them.

While you are connecting with a support system the one thing I would admonish you to be careful of is creating a false "busyness" to cope with the void of a relationship loss. A false busyness is a dangerous trap that many people get into, over working themselves and not really healing at all. A relationship can be over 2, 4, 6, 8 years plus but because you have not taken the time to grieve during the passing of that relationship, the emotional effects of delayed grief can both be a shock and emotionally crippling.

## Step Seven: Free Yourself

When you have experienced a broken relationship one of the first inclinations that most people have is to blame themselves after the break up. It doesn't matter if you were at fault for the break up or not, what you need to do is no free yourself from the responsibility of that relationship. It's now over, you have the release the attachments and the power you gave that relationship and realign your life in a new order. Look at the end of your marriage like this, "its dead". When a dead body is discovered and there is often no known cause to how the person may have died they perform what it called an "autopsy". They cut a sample out of the body for testing to see what the result or cause of death may have been. Your marriage is a relationship that has been cut away from you, it's dead now. The autopsy is over, your autopsy may reveal the cause of death but there's nothing you can do to bring that body back to life again. You may mourn for a season but eventually you have to get back to living again.

When you have suffered a broken marriage the only trouble you can take responsibility for are the problems you created, you cannot take responsibility for your spouse's actions. While you're in the throes of a divorce it's easy to start blaming yourself for everything that took place in the marriage and feeling like you were not good enough for perfect enough.

The truth is, you're really not good enough or perfect enough. In fact, sometimes the guilt were feeling is a result from knowing there were areas we refuse to change in or give more effort to change. Sometimes we know our attitude was off and we did it on purpose, we know we didn't always invest the mental and emotional and sometimes sexual energy that may have brought on the actions of a cheating spouse or an unhappy marriage.

The truth is, not all marriages end because of cheating. Some couples emotionally outgrow each other, there are many reasons for that, people pick people in stages of their lives when they have not fully developed and when they become complete in a career, ministry, business ethic or life style the person they are married to no longer fits the vision of what they want to come home to. It's like living with a roommate and not a soul mate.

Now it's perfectly fine after divorce to question yourself and where your involvement might have played a role in the deterioration of the marriage. Yet ultimately **_you are not responsible for the affair_**. If your marriage deteriorated over financial matters, given the cards you have been dealt there may have been little you could have done to improve or change the situation. That's where communication and compromise come in. If you're not working at all and haven't made an attempt to be a financial help or contributor in your marriage that is now a side of you, you must deal with. You may not be able to go back and fix a bitter marriage that has ended in that case but you can improve your life and be sure that the next time your ship comes in you don't dock at the same landscape.

Freeing yourself means so much on many levels that we can spend the next ten pages explaining how to unravel your life from a divorce but that's not what I want to do. I just want to drop a conversation on you. I just want to drop some wisdom on you and allow you to digest it and process it out in your own life. I may not hit every point that someone might feel should be covered and again I really don't plan to. Freeing yourself means that with or without fault I let it all go. After I have assessed the damages of my emotions, my life, my family, friendships and the like I cannot get stuck at my break up date. You can't stop living at your divorce date. You have to pick up and fall in love with yourself all over again.

Another part of freeing yourself maybe from what we call the "tell tell signs" that your spouse is cheating. You may develop a feeling in the pit of your stomach that something is not right but you can't quite figure out what that feeling is about. Your spouse has become distant, he/she is working late on a regular basis or, maybe your spouse has moved out of the house with no explanation as to why.

You suspect there maybe someone else in their life but every time you bring it up the signs and your spouse denies the possibility. The worst thing you can do is flip out at this point, as hard as that might be, just stay calm and work on communicating a probable cause. Wouldn't it be interesting to find that your spouse is not cheating at all but under stress and wants to distance themselves for relief?

Sometimes we don't take in consideration the atmosphere we set in our home and in a marriage. Atmosphere is one of the problematic areas I had to deal with in my marriage. I was used to my own space being a man who dated and came home to my own space and never had to share it with anyone. While being married I came home to constant yelling and screaming at the kids. I came home to a wife who took about 2-3 hours to acknowledge I was home because she would be in and out of every room in the house talking on the phone and my presence look like it barely mattered. The person experiencing this as well as the person practicing the behavior both need to be mindful of their actions. It is here in marriages where emotional surrogates are born, people turning to a listening ear and before you know it an affair is started and you have no idea how.

Freeing yourself from your past marriage means to let go completely. You can't hold old feelings. You have to find an outlet. You might have to sit with a counselor and talk about it. You might have to write a book, diary or journal, whatever you do get it out. Writing is a cathartic practice that will give you the ability to express emotions that have been pinned up and may not otherwise have an outlet.

You have to forgive, in the process of freeing yourself. How can you not forgive yet expect someone to forgive you when you have done wrong. Wrong is wrong and when the shoe is on the other foot, meaning yours, you're looking for sympathy.

Forgiving will release bitterness and allot of other unhealthy emotions that will try to harbor in your life and take root. Forgiving will make your healing process a real healing and not an emotional bandage that has the potential to reopen.

My last words of advice on freeing yourself would be to "take no prisoners". We have often heard the cliché used by people; depending the conversation or its use it could mean different things. When it comes to freeing yourself taking no prisoners means not harboring no raw emotions. You have to purge out negative attitudes, doubts, bitterness, anger and any other madness that would try to surface from your ex-marriage. I am I promising that any of it is easy? No, not by far, it's going to take some work on your part, mentally, emotionally, spiritual work!

## Chapter Six:

## Symptoms of A Marriage Breakdown

*Open your eyes; you're like a deer caught in headlights. Michael McCain-*

There are some "tell tell signs" or should I say warning signs that a marriage is going sour. You may feel you have "intuition" but as I have explained before having zeal with no knowledge is not always wise. Sometimes you have to allow yourself to be the responsible adult in the situation you're in when you know you want to cut loose and act a fool. Just remain calm through the process because acting out will only put you, your children or others involved in danger. In the end you want to come out of it with as little damage as possible.

Here are some signs and symptoms I've outlined for you as check points for a marriage breakdown.

### 1. *"I love you, but I'm not in love with you"*
No married person would ever imagine hearing those words during the course of their marriage. Yet those very words are usually the conversation starter for a marriage break up or divorce. I can remember when confronting my ex-wife about our marriage her words and excuses for infidelity was that she had fell out of love with me, there was no way that we could even work on our marriage because she no longer had a love for me. My response was there's no way you marry someone and one day wake up and just lose all compassion for your marriage and relationship. I could not fathom that this was what was happening to me.

When you hear that phrase of words, "I love you but I'm not in love with you". Those words are consistent things an already cheating spouse would say. It's part of their personal release of guilt that they can now let go of the present relationship to move fully into whatever their personal plans have become without holding a marriage as a hang-up or responsibility.

If your spouse comes to you stating these words my best advice to you is to believe them! Don't go into denial thinking that it would go away on its own and things would turn around. It won't, face the music. If your spouse is willing to try counseling, that maybe the last lifeline to saving the marriage, If your spouse is unwilling to try counseling there may be very little your efforts will do to turn the situation around. Rather than emotionally and mentally wearing yourself thin, give them what they are asking for, FREEDOM! Let them go, sometimes giving them what they want will also show them they never wanted it in the first place, after a fling does not work out or they decided to come back after guilt and problems whip them into shape it will ultimately be your choice on what you will do with this relationship.

### 2. *"We are just friends"*
Now if your anything like me your already saying to yourself how do you go from being intimate lovers to "just being friends"? Yet couples end on this note all the time. Married couples are in serious danger when a spouse goes from being your intimate love and companion to placing you in the "just friends" category. I could remember in my early years of dating and relationships if I was interested in a young lady I never wanted to hear "we are just friends" or "I view you as a brother to me". Those words nearly killed my self-esteem when it came to dating and relationships and it was not something I wanted to hear from someone who I found to be endearing. Some marriages end on the "we are just friends" note and becomes very confusing for the loving spouse who never saw it coming. The we are just friends would actually sound more like, "I've been thinking about our marriage and lately I've been feeling like we are better off as friends then being in a relationship".

Well if that didn't get you going by now, another and final example of this would be the spouse that comes to you and says, " remember before we got married we promised each other that no matter what we go through, we will always remain friends right?" Directly after hearing those words they bring down the hammer on you. Unexpected you're faced with a fixed decision. Why? Because if you didn't see it coming, this person had plenty of time to think about their way of escape and build a plan for how they would do it. You unfortunately are left to decide how to live your life after the news.

Now the more common tone of "we are just friends" usually stems from a cheating spouse who has what we call "a special friend" they spend allot of time with. If your spouse is spending more and more time with this new "friend" then there is a probably more to it that a mere friendship, you might want to check that out. In reality this "friendship" or "blind attraction" may have started off in pure innocence but after indulging in the emotional gratification your spouse's awareness is not dim that there's a probability there for them to cheat if they have not already acted out on it.

When your spouse develops a close companion outside of your marriage or mutual friends, it usually stems from activities and things they love doing, they may feel they have things in common and like to spend time in those activities or things since they both have a liking for it. I would suggest be careful with this activity. I often suggest to married people to always participate in things with your mate that you don't like, it's a level of compromise, but it also pleases your mate and shows them how much you love and care for them. They know that it's not your cup of tea but the fact that you showed a compromise or interest in something they love is both a turn on and a cause to bring the couple closer. Be careful of people who enter into your spouse's live who have more in common with them then you do. They are active in their lives doing favors that you felt you could not do, or participating in areas you often show no interest in. It's a quick "tell tell" sign that no matter if their interested or not, someone indeed is.

### *3. A sudden need for privacy.*
When I think back on my first marriage I could remember when there was no problem picking up my wife's cell phone to call my parents and see how they were doing or to just use it to call a friend. Everything we shared, it was open and it was like second nature. Later when things began to change there were some behavior adjustments that came as a bit of a shock to me. Suddenly her cell phone was locked and you needed a pass word just to get into it to make phone calls. Then there were the sudden changes of passwords to online accounts and etc.

If you are experiencing this is your marriage its sign that something is going wrong. The sudden need for privacy may be to cover up private emails, text messages, bill payments or charges that they may not want to see on their bank statement or credit cards. I even remember when my ex-wife stopped mail from coming to my house and sent it to a relative's house. So I would not have any idea of what was coming to her in the mail. Now mail may look like nothing big to some people, but letters from the doctor's office about appointments and etc. often came in the mail, when I would question how are things with the doctor I was never allowed to know; which is a big warning sign for someone who is married.

Later in my marriage I found out that my suspicion about the mail could have not been more dead-on. One day a clinic made a mistake about a letter that was being sent to my wife about a scheduled abortion that she had planned with her clinic. An abortion I knew nothing about, not because we didn't want children. As a matter of fact because of the stress we were experiencing in our marriage allot of out intimacy had stopped. At that time there would be no possible way that the pregnancy she terminated would have been my child. I had to live with situations like these that kept amounting up until it all grew out of control. You don't have to live under those conditions. If you know something is wrong in your marriage work it out.

Communication is the biggest key to success in your marriage. You should make your spouse comfortable enough to share anything with you, even if it's something terribly wrong that they might have to share. Nothing should be coming upon you as a shock.

### *4. "I need some space to figure out my feelings"*
When your spouse asked for space in a marriage this of course is dangerous but it's not always a "tell tell sign" of cheating. It maybe for space to think about how to make your relationship better and they may be taking blame for areas in the relationship that needs improvement. Or if you're commonly a couple that argues they may need some space to figure out how to confront you with issues about

your marriage that need serious work. This is an opportunity for self-evaluation to ask yourself why your spouse would feel more comfortable separating from you then laying their issues out on the table to be worked out. It's a sign to you, there are some emotional and communication issues that need to be worked on.

More commonly when you hear from your spouse "I need some space to figure out my feelings" it's a sign they have emotionally moved on, their cheating or entertaining the idea of moving on. If your spouse has cheated, thinking about it or want to move on because the relationship is becoming overwhelming you still have a chance of saving your marriage if you work at it. There are many marriages that grow stronger after infidelity because both spouses now understand what they have in their marriage. The cheating spouse knows they don't deserve a second chance and is often willing to do right with this chance rather than mess it up again.

More often than not when you hear those words, "I need space" it's usually some feelings of confusion that your spouse may have about your relationship and the potential of another relationship that may have surfaced. It's not always that every person jumps up and cheats, your spouse may literally be entertaining the thought of moving on but separating themselves from you, your family and children might give them the clarity of thought they have been looking for on deciding what to do. It may also be a sign that your spouse is trying to figure out ways of creating freedom so they can explore moments with this new "friend" or blatant relationship unbeknown to you.

### 5. Sudden change in friendships and associates
One of the things I notice my ex-wife would do when she wanted space and time to do her thing was she would suddenly change up on the people she commonly associated with. Sometimes I knew where to find her if she was not home and who I could call that would always know where she would be. When she was in her cheater mode those habits suddenly changed and not only that sources could no longer be trusted as some of them where often given the heads up about what was happening. She would change the people she handed out with, as there were some people I would commonly trust her with because I knew she was safe and there was no suspicion surrounding them.

Once she gained my trust with certain friendships, she then changed things and I was unaware who she would really be hanging with. Or she would be vague about where she was going or what she was doing. I couldn't really say she was lying because she would be sure not to specify too much detail but just what she thought I needed to know.

### 6. Regular work habits change.
Sudden and sporadic changes in work habits can become a sign that something is going on. Now, let me make one thing clear just because your spouse maybe "doing overtime" at work may not always be

a lie, so before you go off on a tangent make sure you are certain of your suspicions.

In my marriage I had to deal with things that became obvious. She wanted to hang out with friends and coworkers I never heard of or met people that were out of the usual. I am the type of person to give people there space and sometimes enough rope to hang themselves. So there was no need for me to follow behind her to check everything she's doing because I know that in time it will all be exposed. The one thing I can tell you is that women are usually better liars and better at cheating then men.

So my advice is to be on the lookout for frisk changes and last minute changes and switches. Sometimes when you're planning to do one thing and things change you pay less attention to what's going on when you are a person or couple with a busy life. I can tell you in my marriage I was guilty of that. I was so busy with my life that at times I could care less of what she was doing. Because I had my instincts about things it furthered my "I don't care" attitude. So your best bet is to know the facts. Never approach your spouse with suspicion, just express the fact you notice the changes and don't particularly care for them, allow them the room to improve and change.

### 7. Spending large amounts of time on the internet or phone:
In today's world technology advances have turned the average cheater into high-tech cheaters. Technology gives the cheater the ability to

communicate with their prospects and dates while on a date with you, sitting in the bed with you or having family moments. While we watch things in movies at times and see how cheaters set up dates and flings while with their wife or husband it's not far off from what actually happens.

When a cheater starts spending a large amount of time on the internet/computer, checking emails and other social networks chances are they have built a connection with someone you might not be aware about. I have seen social networks destroy marriages and potential marriages because people communicate with ex-boyfriends, girlfriends, husbands and wives, high school lovers and so on. Before you know it something very innocent can turn into cheating. Some people cannot handle the temptation well, others want the attention and fall prey. No matter what side of things you end up on set some boundaries for yourself with emails and social networking. Some couples even choose to avoid it all together, the choice is yours.

In today's world affairs are started with online dating sites, quick texting to someone you met at work, on the train or while shopping. People start forming secret email accounts, trying to hide their "other life" and keep it out of sight from their spouse. A large number of cheaters when asked why they find it necessary to go beyond their committed relationship will usually say they were "emotionally" involved with the person first. The person listened to them, seemed to care for them, did favors they could not get there spouse to do, they were emotionally supportive of them and before long, they became sexually involved.

If you catch your spouse chatting online excessively, hanging out in chat rooms and visiting pornographic websites then you have reason to be concerned. You have all the symptoms of a cheating spouse with wondering eyes or a wondering heart looking for a new fling. It's time to put your plan in place for how you will address the issue, before going off assess the damages. You may have a marriage that can survive your infidelity when you handle the situation correctly. If you have made up your mind to break free, do it peacefully.

## 8. *Behavior that does not add up*
When you have a family or dating routine and all of a sudden things become interrupted without legitimate proof or explanation, beware. When you wife or husband is not where you expect them to be and missing time that really can't be explained, look out. Or how about you find yourself going through bank statements and receipts and notice charges or payments for stuff you don't have or own. Missing clothing, clothing that doesn't belong to anyone in your family but winds up in your car or with the family clothes to be washed by accident. Finding extra clothes is an age old trick that allot of cheating women will do as a test to see if their man is with someone else besides them. They will leave underwear in unsuspecting places in hopes that someone, particularly the woman would find it.

Some women and men have fetishes, so finding memorabilia, pictures, items of clothing or other that you have never seen before are all warning signs to what may be happening with your spouse.

Sudden arguments about you or your children using their phone, answering their calls or using their computers when there never seem to ever have been a problem before. Last but not least just begin caught in a constant web of lies about where they were or how the day's events were for them. A slip up in details or sudden changes in the story or people reporting they ran into them when they should have been elsewhere.

### 9. *The phone*
Secretive phone calls and more time spent on the phone then what should be.
Or how about excessive texting to people or so called "friends" you never met or heard of before. These are usually one of the tell sings that something is going wrong in your marriage. I can remember telling my ex-wife "a conversation that can't be hand in front of me or in my presence is a conversation that should not be had". Some people viewed it as me being a controlling husband but my suspicions were already at an all-time high with plenty of evidence to back it up.

Emotional affairs often primarily occur via the phone, especially cell phones. A spouse who's cheating will never be able to have a conversation in front of you on the phone with the person. Texting is something different, most phone screens are not large enough to see the writing depending where you're sitting or standing. So texting right under your nose is not unusual, using the phone to talk is a different story. When you notice your spouse has the leave the room to have conversations or hanging up the phone suddenly when you enter the room. With today's technology you can lock cell phones and place codes on them so they can't be open. If you don't know the code you can't use the phone. Locked cell phones are not really the problem; it's when you don't have the password to get in. Or how about when they finish making phone calls you notice they delete their phone history or becoming defensive when asked about it, you might want to check phone records.

10. **_Your personal intuition_**
If all of a sudden in your relationship you're plagued with the feeling of fear, worry, impatience, doubt and anxiety of about your spouse's actions or whereabouts chances are it's your own intuition warning you. I personally believe most people have intuition while some use it others don't. It was personal dreams I would have a night that were totally supernatural for me that began to reveal what my cheating wife was doing, while I had no physical evidence I believe what I saw. I used that information to prove it, confront her, only to be told I was "crazy" and a liar making up these people, places and events.

If you find yourself looking for excuses on why your spouse maybe cheating then it's time for you to look for further evidence and proof. Just because you may be having your doubts and suspicion does not mean that they are legitimate. Find the proof first. Most people waste time by trying to give themselves reasons why their spouse is not cheating or why they would never cheat. You really never know what a person would or wouldn't do, you're never above cheating, and it happens to even the most unsuspecting people. Take time to talk to your spouse once you have gathered your facts, tell them what you have found and why it bothers you. Be ready for the lies, they will come. Be ready to ask for honesty, it's a fact that people who have affairs try their luck at becoming excellent liars. Stay calm and courteous, remember your goal is to get the truth, even if it hurts prepare yourself for what you might hear.

# Chapter Seven:

## Marriage Infidelity

*True love is faithful when one party is absent or both are present. You don't cheat because you're fully committed.*

*Michael McCain-*

When it comes to the topic of infidelity the word itself leaves a bad taste in your mouth. A breach of trust in a relationship is often one of the hardest blows you can recover from. Yet not all marriages with infidelity end in the sour note of divorce. Some people are strong willed and do whatever they deem possible to make it recover. Many people feel like they don't have the emotional strength to pick up and move on, some people are just plain ole tired of starting all over again. It's a process that becomes wearing on your when you have been in a few unsuccessful relationships no matter who was at fault.

When you suffer infidelity the hardest question to ask yourself is… will my marriage survive infidelity? If your marriage survives the blow of infidelity is dependent on many different things. One of the major things is the restoration of trust. If trust is to be restored to your marriage the cheater must be willing to cooperate with you and give you the grounds you feel are certain to rebuild trust to restore that marriage. Most men can relate to this, because women often say men are not the best cheaters and often get caught, partly true but what women don't understand is that most of the time the man as already replaced you and really does not care if he was caught or not. Timing when caught cheating plays the major difference.

The hard part of restoring a relationship after infidelity is restoring trust but with that trust comes all the information on what happen in that affair. I would suggest taking some counseling and getting a mediator to help work out the details and provide some sensible advice on how to heal from the process of finding out into the process of restoring if you really intend for it to work. The cheater has to then be genuinely remorseful for their behavior in order for there to be a change and real success afterward.

So looking for an apology does not mean the man is really sorry or the woman is really sorry. People have used up apologies and we learned early in life that when you do something wrong you just say sorry and it will make it all go away, but that's so far from the truth but it's a mindset that we have been taught form our early years in life. How many times have you been wrong in your life and just thought that a simple apology would make it all better. Sometimes people feel like if people don't render an apology right away their not truly sorry. Sometimes it takes some thought into what went wrong and placing yourself in the other person shoes to really see how they feel and a genuine apology might come out of that. Not just an "I am sorry" but a real change!

I am not a real fan of divorce, but sometimes you have to do what you have to do. Marriages can survive infidelity under certain circumstances. Shortly I will share with you some examples of how I think a marriage can survive the blow of infidelity and come out strong. Sometimes these hardships show couples how much they are meant for each other and how much they truly love each other.

Case One: Emotional Surrogates:

I have seen marriages end over spouses building emotional surrogates to help cope with something lacking in their relationship or just because they may have found the person attractive but knowing they can't go in to a full affair they will use this person for fantasy, emotional support, a "friend", confidant or even dating, going places and spending time with them that they may not be able to do with their spouse. Needless to explain that emotional surrogates are a dangerous relationship to get into but it does not stop people from trying it out.

In today's society emotional cheating happens almost every day. People develop fetishes and habits that they feed or want others to feed. For example, many couples are struggling with what they now call "Sexting" which is sending comments and pictures by phone to a friend or stranger talking about sex. Some do it for the attention and the affection that they feel they are not getting. Sometimes it's even the high that they feel from doing it and not getting caught. Some extreme cases of "sexting" goes beyond comments in a text message or pictures, it includes videos as well as our phones over the last few years have advance greatly.

Besides the world of sexting there's the online community of websites some for sex and dating, others can be as common as Facebook and YouTube. People have learned to take any account and do what they want with it. While social media has its benefits it also has its down side. I personally believe two adults need to be mature enough to trust each other and know the value of what they have in a relationship. I've see couples get into heated arguments over comments and emails people send to them, it's even happened in my relationships and I had to explain to the person I was dating that I can't control the things people say, you don't have to flirt with people to make them flirt with you. Sometimes the more you try to make it clear you're not available the more they are turned on by the case.

So can your marriage survive emotional surrogacy? Of course it can, yet there are people that in their anger that will end relationships because they cannot contend with the thought that their spouse can entertain friendships or conversations outside of their marriage. A remedy to help deal with problems like this is to set boundaries, work on intimacy in your own relationship, get some personal counseling to help with the problem should you really notice that there is one.

Case Two: One Night Stand:
If the infidelity/affair was a one-time occurrence and your spouse is genuinely remorseful, your marriage can survive the infidelity. If your spouse was caught in a one night stand or confessed their involvement in a one night stand then chances are your marriage could actually survive that experience. You will know how to handle this situation when it happens although you may be hurt or upset by it. Your spouse caught in a onetime affair will genuinely be remorseful; your marriage can survive the infidelity. Now I don't make excuses for people who have slip up and mishaps in their marriage. I myself can't really judge anyone because I am far from perfect, we all mess up sometimes.

I can remember counseling a young 18 year old who was talking about getting married and fresh out of my previous marriage, I was his age when I had planned to get married and I did. Now we all know that marriage was not successful and some might say I was talking out of my pain but I would rather say I was talking out of my experience. I can remember telling the young man "at your age you are entitled to at least one bad relationship, but don't let it be your marriage". When you're young you're still exploring your life, you put up with things that older adults will not tolerate. When you're dating you are learning things about yourself, your temperament, your abilities, the type of women you like or interested in. I think the mistake most men and even women make in dating and relationships is conjoining themselves to a person they think is moldable and pliable, someone they think they can change and shape into the person they want them to be.

A one night stand, as sticky as the situation is it is forgivable if the person show they are really remorseful for it. If you can't identify they are truly sorry for it, then you are taking a chance you will later regret. I can remember I would confront my ex-wife with information, or out of "intuition" of knowing something was happening and I would be right, she showed no remorse for it and I then was left on my own to decide what I would do from there. Would I forgive her or would I let the marriage go. Nobody should live in a marriage where you have to decide week to week or month to month if you want to continue being married or not.

Yet we are all flawed, as much as your expect the best of your mate they are still capable of messing up as you are. If we just tell the truth for a moment, you would mess up too if the right opportunity was before you. I hear allot of people say I would not cheat, I personally call them all liars because if the right stuff was before you, walking talking, looking, smelling, shaped and presenting everything you like and want it would cross your mind how you could get away with it. Being flawed human beings who make mistakes, we are deserving of second chances. Working together as a couple to fix the problem could mean ending up with a stronger bond and better marriage than you had before the cheating and infidelity.

Case Three: Midlife Crisis:

There's something strange about a midlife crisis that in your younger years of marriage people look at differently. When you're younger and go through divorce people look at you as if you're dirty, unclean and did something so sinful or disrespectful to your mate to be in that situation. When your older and in your forties and pushing fifty years old, people look at you as if your just desiring a change of life. While that may all be partially true, the age has little to do with it. The desire you have at forty-something is no different from the young couple in their twenties and thirties.

What happens with a cheating spouse in a midlife crisis is mainly a mental and emotional experience. In your midlife crisis, a person wants to know they are still attractive, still desired, still loved and people still view them as sharp and sexy as they did in the prime of their life. At this stage it doesn't make it acceptable, but if this is the cause for why your mate is looking for attention and affection outside of the marriage, this is a case that your marriage can still survive the infidelity.

Case Four: Drugs or Alcohol:

We all know that there's nothing good about drugs and alcohol, but there's an apparent truth connected to it when it comes to cheating. If your spouse has been drinking or using drugs it has the ability to impair their thoughts and actions. Now being under the influence of drugs or alcohol is not an excuse for bad behavior, yet drugs and alcohol can influence certain people to do things they would not normally do. If your spouse engages in infidelity while under the influence of drugs or alcohol you should take into consideration whether it was your spouse driving the behavior of the drugs or alcohol.

We have all heard crazy stories about spouses getting drunk or using drugs and cheating. Now the question is was this drugs and alcohol used by someone on them or were they in the wrong place at the wrong time where their inability to think rationally was taken advantage of. The last question you should ask yourself is this repeated behavior? Once maybe forgivable but a repeat offender of the same behavior or excuse renders a complete different story.

## Forgiveness & Infidelity

When it comes to the topic of forgiveness with a cheating marriage I can hear people saying yeah, yeah, yeah, I heard all of that gibberish before and very few people authentically forgive after a case of infidelity. Sometimes it takes years to unravel all the memories, buildup of emotions and move into progression. Forgiveness is like age; you can grow older but not mature. Just because you're old doesn't mean you are mature. Forgiveness is a paradigm that is metaphorically the same. Just because you are out of a relationship does not mean you're healed from it. Even if you're walking around confessing I am over it, done with it and want nothing to do with it. In my next chapter I will see if you have what it takes to forgive your cheating spouse and stay in that marriage and heal. Are you ready?

Diary Of An Ex-Husband

# Chapter Eight:

## Infidelity & Stages of Recovery

*True Love Is Unconditional. Michael McCain-*

According to recent statistics about 5% of every thousand will end their marriage in divorce. While that number may not seem large lets set the record even more clear, in the U.S. 49% of marriage end each year, making the U.S. one of the leading countries in the divorce statistics. Ironically 50% of Christian marriages end in divorce in comparison to Non-Christian homes. No matter if you're a faith based family or not, everyone seems to be experiencing changes at this thing we call "family". It's easy to sit pointing the finger trying to speculate who has it right. It's an apparent fact that people on both ends of the game are being effected and no one has all the right answers because each of us are flawed being aiming to reach a percentage of perfection.

If you have been an un-faithful wife or husband I have taken the time to put together and outline of steps you could take to recover from infidelity in your marriage but you have to remember that both parties have to want it and be willing to work on it to assure that it will work out for the best. If you still have ties to your fling or lover, it and your husband or wife is willing to let go of the fact you cheated to save your marriage by all means that is the time to get rid of the person and cut ties to save your family or marriage.

The steps in these recovery methods I am sharing with you appeal largely to a woman who is caught cheating and a husband who is trying to understand steps needed to be taken to strengthen and save a broken marriage. These same steps I am sharing with you are no different than any steps that should be taken if it were a man cheating on his wife trying to save and fix a marriage so please give me some room to help the women, but there is still some helpful advice in here for the men as well, so open your heart and take it all in.

## Steps to Recovery:

**1. Honesty**

The first extraordinary precaution to avoid your lover (the person you committed your affair and infidelity with) then tell your husband all about your affair, and the decision you have made to restore your love for him. Then promise to keep telling him the truth about every aspect of your life, so you never again have a secret second life where you are tempted to hurt him behind his back. This will help give him the grounds needed to build trust back in the relationship and look forward to giving it another chance. If your spouse does not feel that your being completely honest about what you have done and what you are currently doing your chances of saving the marriage will quickly drift.

Honesty and openness is one of the best ways to prevent yourself from being inconsiderate of your husband's feelings. I can remember in my marriage I was honest enough with my wife to admit to her when other women would flirt too much with me. I wad daring and honest enough to admit when I felt tempted or when I felt I was losing interest in our marriage even though it was still a new marriage. This may seem harsh or come across as bad, but it is honest and I always gave my wife a fighting chance to save her marriage before allowing myself to wonder physically or emotionally. Needless to say I had no idea that I was in my marriage alone because my wife had her own game going on the entire time. Yet when it became nearly too late and I began to shut down and show less of the love and attention I used to give, it alarmed her and she began to show change.

Another thing you should consider about confronting your spouse about infidelity is never to put a friend in the middle of what you are doing. You may have a friend that knows all your secrets, knows who your with when your there, knows the person you cheating with, but you should never put anyone in the middle of helping you explain reasons as to why you were unfaithful in your marriage. You should not boost a friend to go to your husband and tell them for you, you should do it yourself. Go right to your husband with the facts. If you had been honest about your budding relationship with your lover from the beginning, it would never have developed into an affair.

Partly these were the reason I exercised being honest about people flirting with me because I saw a door open. It didn't matter if I was interested in the person or not. I knew that some people had it out for me anyway and would love to do anything not to have me but to prove there was nothing to my marriage to begin with. So out of respect as a man I did what most men say is going too far. Some men like the extra attention, makes them feel sexy and needed. In some cases they will use that attention to their advantage and maybe even fantasize about being with the person or use them as an emotional escape form a troubled or not so fiery marriage.

# Diary Of An Ex-Husband

You may be afraid that once your husband knows the facts about your ongoing affair (or maybe you ended your affair early because you felt convicted, it's all the same), he will leave you. The fear of letting your husband in on the truth will always be tempting to keep the affair going or to continue hiding it. Your best bet is to end it while you can and come clean about it. You might be scared that your husband will leave you; quite frankly, I think he has the right to make that decision.

If, faced with the facts he decides to divorce you, you lose your option to restore your relationship with him. You can count your losses at the point but still make an effort to ask for forgiveness and at least end your marriage peaceably especially if you have children involved in the marriage. If your husband decides to end the marriage, it may be a tough call but the reality is you simply cannot build a relationship on lies and deception. Dishonesty will never get you to your goal of loving your husband again. So it's better to get all of the cards out on the table now and build your marriage the right way, even if there is a chance that your husband will throw in the towel before you have a chance to reconcile.

Another reason you may be reluctant to tell your husband the truth is that he might have a violent reaction to what you have done. Even if your husband has never shown a temper before you still may wonder if this would be the spark of something you're not prepared for. If you are afraid of his reaction, separate from him first, and then tell him the truth in a public place or with friends who can protect you. You may want to invite him to meet with a counselor while breaking the news to him to assure your own safety; sometimes friends and family my agitate the situation and make it worse when breaking news of that type. If your husband cannot control his temper once he knows the facts, then I see no hope of saving your marriage. Honesty is so important in marriage that if the threat of violence prevents honesty, I don't believe you will ever have a good marriage.

Some women choose to continue hiding their infidelity and affairs because they feel they will end all chances of saving their marriage. Better yet they may hurt their husband or bring anger, violence and rage out of him they have never seen before. Dishonesty does not prevent violence in a marriage, it encourages it. The only result you will gain from continuing to be dishonest about you infidelity is that you just may enrage him even the more to find out on his own that you are cheating or that you have been lied this entire time he thought you were faithful.

If you think your husband may divorce you or become violent when you are honest with him, I encourage you to be honest anyway, before you begin your plan for reconciliation. If he cannot accept the truth, no plan of reconciliation will work.

## 2. Account for Your Time.

Once you have established a willingness to be completely honest with your husband, you should then continue to be honest with him about all of your activities. Make sure he knows about everything you do throughout the day. Give him a complete schedule of your activities, and let him know which of those activities make you most tempted to contact your former lover. Some people may say it's a bit extreme but you are the cheater remember? So if you want to rebuild trust and regain the grounds necessary to save your marriage and relationship your best bet is to put it all out there on the table and even be ready to answer some of his questions repeatedly because they may resurface. If you husband is asking questions again and again, chances are he's looking for a lie and wants to totally trust that everything you have told him so far is the absolute truth.

You have to be honest about what tempts you to go see your lover so you can cut the ties. You also have to be honest about it if you intend to give your husband a fighting chance to be able to help you pull back the pieces from this infidelity to save your marriage. This will strengthen his trust and now your job will ultimately be to avoid people and places that increase your craving to be with him.

## 3. Spend As Much of Your Time with Your Husband as Possible.

When the truth comes out there will sometimes be a feeling of withdrawal. You want to avoid that much as possible not to go back into you old habits or trying to reconnect with your lover. Your best bet is to stick it out and know that it will be uncomfortable, but right now it's really not the fact if you're comfortable because you brought this harm into the relationship so you need to focus on rebuilding it. Understand it may take your husband sometime to forgive and open back up in the way he used to. In some cases I have seen people that love harder because of their spouse's honesty about their cheating and they were able to fix a broken marriage and relationship.

In many cases, I have suggested that a husband and wife go on a three-week vacation together during the first few weeks of withdrawal, just to help the wayward spouse avoid contacting the former lover. I tell these couples not to expect too many passionate moments to happen, because your husband may still be emotionally recovering. Your husband may not be too warm towards showing affection but maybe something that can be worked on, don't force it. By getting away from the reminders of the lover, for a time may help the healing process to begin. There will be much work that goes into that process but you ultimately want to show your husband you're serious about separating and putting all that's in the past in the past for good.

I have talked to couples who never understood why going away would help save the marriage. It helps to lessen the effects that happen with withdrawal and helps to focus in on the areas of the marriage that needs rebuilding. Besides, the distractions of a vacation can often compensate for the depression that accompanies withdrawal, and makes the experience much less painful.

I have seen cases where the cheater wanted to go away saying they needed time to regroup themselves and pull themselves back together after revealing that they were unfaithful to their spouse. If wayward spouse feels like getting away from everyone during withdrawal and going on the vacation alone; I want you to know right now, it usually doesn't work. It's too tempting to call the lover, and in many cases the lover ends up joining the wayward spouse. You will end up at square one all over again. I can tell you from experience that I have took time away thinking I needed to calm myself as an angry husband because of finding out what my wife was doing. All it really did was create more time and space for her to do more of what she had been doing with her lover (and in my case lovers).

Going away on vacation with your husband will help the two to talk out all the things that need to be said and spend some time bonding again. Don't expect to be intimate with your husband or even to have desires to be intimate because you will be learning during that time how to purge out your addiction and strong desires for your lover and refocus in on loving your husband and saving the marriage. The feeling for intimacy will come again once the two rebuild the bond that needs to exist in order to go further. Don't make the mistake of trying to use sex to heal the marriage because it may disgust your husband even the more, there will be times where he can't help but think about the fact that you have been intimate with someone else and it will take some time for him to heal from those thoughts.

Of course on the other end of things your husband should take the time to help you heal even though he was the one the received the offense against him. I am sure he will be tempted to throw up your cheating ways in your face from time to time, that's almost to be expected. If your husband is serious he will respect your feelings knowing that making comments or smart remarks will only keep the wound fresh and cause the healing process to take longer. It may also be wise for any man in this state to tame his tongue not to give reason for your spouse to retreat back to their old ways.

**4. Avoid Slip Ups**

While your whole heart should be focused on fixing the marriage and saving it, God forbid you slip up again, or even be tempted just to see your lover or call them, admit that to you husband quickly and be honest about it. This does not lessen the fact that you have either done it or have been thinking about it but will again give him the fighting chance needed to get a grip on the marriage. After taking all those precautions try including things to keep you from slipping up again. Keep improving them until it becomes virtually impossible for you to contact your lover. A slip will set you back emotionally, but it does not mean that your recovery plan has been ruined. It simply needs an upgrade. Stick to your plan, make adjustments to it as needed and keep moving forward.

In some cases relocating to a new city, state or getting away from a surrounding area where your lover is located or resides might be worth the move in saving your marriage. Some may think it's an extreme move, but how serious are you about saving your marriage? When you count up the cost it I am sure your heart will tell you its well worth the move. It's a good example of an extraordinary precaution upgrade, when it became apparent that contact with a lover could not be avoided when living in the same city. It goes without saying that when lovers are fellow employees, a job change is absolutely essential to marital recovery. It would be easy to think that this is not possible but in most cases that's usually where a spouse finds a lover outside their marriage. When you think about it for a moment it makes sense how you make friends at work, take lunch breaks together, helping each other with assignments and some may have had it in their intentions all along to get involved and enjoy the game while risking your marriage.

**5. What if my fling started at my work place?**

How is total separation from a former lover possible when you work together? This is where the conversation need to happen or the consideration of a total job switch will come into play. Your goal is to save your marriage and to break ties with your former lover. Your spouse needs to also be at peace that nothing will present itself to revisit that relationship.

**6. Stay away from other methods that tempt you**

You need not for me to tell you we live in the age of technology and your spouse could be communicating with a fling by text, email, web cam and several other methods you're your serious about fixing and saving your marriage then you already know my answer to this step. You should avoid any avenue that could lure you into communication with your lover until you have fully recommitted to your spouse, gotten over the withdrawal from your lover and your emotions are now all back in tact where they should be. You can always return to email, social networking sites and etc. when you have rebuilt your marriage back to the place it should be and gotten over your fling.

## Chapter Nine:

## Five Rules To Guide Marital Recovery

*"Recovery starts with honesty".*

*Michael McCain-*

Before we reach the end of this book I want to share with you five basic yet extremely important keys or what I would like to refer to as rules. These rules while they may seem basic are the key building blocks to saving and rebuilding a marriage after infidelity. If you follow these steps and work on them no matter if infidelity has exist in your marriage or not it will help bring your marriage to a great bond and help you grow together as a couple. After all if the two of you love each other you will work hard on doing everything in your power to save your marriage and family.

These are the Five Rules to Guide Marital Recovery a marriage that has experienced infidelity should follow to help you restore your love for each other:

# The Five Rules:

1. Protect your marriage
2. Care for your marriage
3. Give Time to your marriage
4. Keep honesty in your marriage
5. Work on keeping the fire in your marriage

When you think about the steps I am providing for you when followed correctly and taken to heart you will understand its importance and how it saves a broken marriage. Let's start with protection. After all letting your guard down and committing infidelity is no easy thing for both the cheater and the person who experiences the offense; But after making the commitment to work on the marriage you may need to take extra precautions' now to protect it. Consider the needs of your spouse and the fact that they are willing to give you the chance needed to save and redeem your marriage. Take that to heart and use that to fuel yourself with the strength you need when you may be weak and wanting to totally give up.

The second step goes hand and hand with it all and that's giving care to your marriage, not just doing things that will give you a setback but learning how to be there for your spouse emotionally. The hardest part for either in the marriage may be getting over the physical blockage and memories from the past relationship. You have to work hard on that, you will experience some withdrawal from a former lover but over time you will also heal and be able to put that completely in your past if you're serious about rebuilding your marriage. Remember that adding care means you make yourself available to your spouse giving them the attention they need mentally, emotionally and physically.

The third is giving time to your marriage; you will have to make sure your making your marriage a priority. Giving the right time to your marriage assuring that you are spending time and as much time with your spouse as needed. If you or your spouse ever feel that time is not being spent in should be corrected, it should be brought up in your time alone and thought about carefully to assure that you don't end but back at square one all over again; time with your spouse and time doing things with family are important key factors to having a strong marriage and a strong family unit.

The fourth step is keeping honesty in your marriage. Honesty, honesty, honesty! I can't stress it enough. Couples have to learn how to be vulnerable and open up to each other. If you don't learn to do that with your spouse and be honest with them you will find yourself developing emotional surrogates. If you develop and emotional surrogate it may not always lead to physical intimacy, you can be emotionally in love with someone hoping to express that passion and desire, or something you may be lacking in your marriage with your spouse. Emotional surrogacy is dangerous and usually leads to outright cheating, which is why honesty needs to be kept in a marriage. Open up to your spouse, let them know your fears, your desires, and your temptation and let them see where your heart is. It's nothing wrong with being honest. Never use your honesty to guide your spouse into doing things they may not want to do. Let them make the decision to make personal changes or try new things or explore fantasies that you may have.

Last but definitely not the least, is working on keeping the fire in your marriage. I know there may be sighs at this point and even some umm hmm's here and there but it is so vitally important to keep the fire in your marriage. Fire does not always mean sex. But what it does mean is that romance is in your marriage. Learn how to express love that does not include sex but maybe a turn on to express sex.

When there's romance in a marriage fire comes almost naturally, there's no extra put on that are needed because each person in the marriage is considering the mental needs, physical needs and emotional needs of the other person in the marriage. Keeping the fire burring is learning that sometimes you can be boring by doing the same thing all the time. Touching your spouse the same way, or having sex all the time in the same positions or etc. are a few examples of what I am speaking of. Keeping the fire in your marriage will teach you how to come up with romantic ideas, vacation ideas, learning how to pitch in around the house and in the family to relieve stress and help make time and maybe provide you with the extra attention you crave or the sex you may feel deprived of.

I know I kept this one short, but its advice straight from my heart and I have used it time and time again in helping other couples redeem or save their troubled marriage. Are you ready to do what it takes to save yours? I am sure there are other steps you can take and other things you can do. I am not promising to be an all-out expert, but largely this book was written of my own personal experience out of areas where I went wrong or needed more help in and that are how I am able to share it with you.

# Diary Of An Ex-Husband

# Chapter Ten:

## Emotional Epiphany

*"An epiphany is simply when your soul exhales". Michael McCain-*

Here's the part most people reading have been waiting for, where I tell my story in a more personal way. I promise you my intent with this book is to keep everything tasteful but to just express what I have gone through. In this chapter I will share with you pages I wrote in my journal about an experience I had with God that helped liberate me from the baggage I was carrying from my former marriage.

Jan. 2, 2011 something I had been waiting for happened! It was such an epiphany it came on all of a sudden and so unexpected. I went out for a walk it was a week after the blizzard of Dec. 2010. I was just taking the time to enjoy the strange weather we had that day, it was windy but not quite cold yet. Temperatures around 50 degrees I was observing

## Diary Of An Ex-Husband

everything around me, just praying in my heart while walking and the strangest thing happen.

While I was walking I stated to feel like I had stepped in something or on something because the bottom of my shoes had begun to feel so uneven and I felt quirky while I was walking. I ignored it for about two to three blocks hoping whatever it was would level out or fall off the bottom of my shoe and I can tell you it didn't, it just began to get all the more annoying. I glanced around me to see if I could gather if it was me walking on the bottom hem of my old navy jeans, as I began to pull my pants up a little higher in hopes that I had found the solution and just a block more the same issue. So as I walked through Catona Park I glanced down and my black timberland boots and began to notice something so strange…

The entire bottom heal collapsed and fell out of my boot. I was staggering trying to attempt to hold myself up. Both with tears in my eyes and laughing with amazement I just wondered "how in the world did that happen?" As I began to walk more the same thing happened to my other heel, as I was already mentally complex and worried about someone noticing I really began to feel just great about what I was dealing with! Needless to say I was deeply embarrassed, yet there was no one there with me. So as I walked I held my head up Tan H&M coat, Tan messenger Coach bag Louis Vuitton Scarf and I walked praying as I had already been doing and I began to tell myself "this just means change"… while I felt something quaking in my bones I could barely explain I then affirmed those words by saying, "my wardrobe is expanding with new and better things"... Yet in reality I need not another item of clothing, I just wanted to reverse the negative thoughts and feelings that so easily began to invade my mind after the reality of my experience.

Walking two to three more blocks up I heard that still small voice speak to me and say, "Are you ready to throw this out?" I literally stopped walking dead center in the middle of the street and shook my head in an up and down motion as if I was saying YES!

What in the world could I be saying yes to? This same voice spoke back and said, "Finally the bottom fell out, and now I am here to catch you!" I then understood that what I was experiencing was far deeper than some Timberland's that dry rotted and fell apart at the bottom. The voice spoke again and again, this time it said to me, "your life has been in this condition for some time now, well-polished on the surface but cracking and falling apart on the inside."

As I walked, it took every fiber of my existence not to cry while I was walking, I felt like I was in the fight of my life. I felt how a child lost in a mall with thousands of people who first realizes that there family is nowhere in sight. I am in the middle of a crowded New York City street and felt like I was smack center in a GOD moment and no one around me would even understand what just happen.

# Let It All Go!

It was at that moment that I understood it was time for me to let go and forgive. Whatever it was I was holding in my heart was no longer important. It was time to forgive my ex-wife, former friends, co-workers, neighbors, relatives and the long list of people who got involved with contributing to my marriage being a mess. I even had to forgive myself. As I walked down the street and arrived closer and closer to my home I could feel my heart physically healing. I knew God had answered my longing prayer to be healed because it was time to let it all go. I forgave in that moment my ex-wife for cheating, her infidelity, he lies, her pretending, her games she played. It all went from me.

There was a part of me that actually wanted to hold on to the pain, I was addicted to the pain. I learned to enjoy being angry. It was how I protected myself. It was how I kept other people from getting close to me. It was how I kept myself from dating and thinking about every marring again. Once I got a grip on my emotions the healing took over me and I could feel the fear leaving me, I could feel the sense of betrayal and abandonment departing from me. I could feel my heart again. For about four years I was walking around numb, I was dead and didn't even have a clue. I had stopped living and was determined to just rot in my existence.

The way I was raised I never planned to ever divorce. I was in it forever, till death do us part. It took allot for me to wrap my mind around living my life without my wife, two sons and picking up the pieces to me all over again. Some of my closest friends and relatives would often say I have a habit of going through things and never processing it. I can admit in this case I was definitely guilty of that fact.

I forgave my ex-wife time and time again when she would not admit to being unfaithful. There were times I was accused of working witchcraft because some information she would not know how I knew it. I would dream things, names and get descriptions of people and she could not accept the fact that I was gifted and God would show me. I had to forgive her for cheating with coworkers and college friend's, even members of the local church. The most dangerous thing I did was trying to stay in a relationship with someone who didn't want it.

My emotions became so numb form the constant go through that I had no fight in me. I thought if I become like her, it would get her attention. So I tried talking to other people to see if she would get jealous, it worked a while but after a while I had to pull myself back together. I notice that from my pain I was trying to become a person I was not. I finally decided to end the marriage and by then she was actually ready to fight, to try. I had lost my fight and I thought about how I didn't want to go through this for the rest of my life.

I later noticed after applying for my divorce and fighting depression that I was no longer interested in dating. When I least expected it another relationship appeared and I thought it would work. I was ready, but because I and this person both went through terrible marriages we could not trust each other and there was allot of misunderstanding. I eventually had to let go, work on healing myself and getting back to my purpose.

# My Final Words

I want to say to every man experiencing saving his marriage, do it with all you got. I also want you to understand that there will be moments when old feelings come up, it would be unfair to you wife to keep holding on to those feelings. You have to learn to forgive. It's easy to become addicted to pain and it becomes all you know. No matter if you staying in the relationship to save it or if you are working on making peace to end it, no matter what side of the game you're on FORGIVE.

The un-forgiveness will block everything you're trying to do. You can become angry, bitter and worst of all ends up in an easy relationship using some other woman to help you heal from your brokenness. There are times those types of relationships work, then there are times you can damage yourself more as well as the person you're in the relationship with. I have heard people say that sometimes as long as you have been in the relationship will be as long as it would take to heal. From my own experience, forgiveness is a lifetime work. You can say you forgive and mean it but every now and then something may surface to show you that you have not honestly forgiven or that challenge is showing you that you truly are healed and you will see how you have grown and matured and it's worth the celebration to be grateful that you made it out with your right mind and your emotions and heart intact.

# Diary Of An Ex-Husband

## Other Books By The Author:

1. Soul Cleanse Vol. 1 (Poetry)
2. Life Editing Vol. 1 (Taking Out The Trash)
3. The Millionaire Class Vol. 1 (The Rules of Engagement to Making Money
4. The Newborn Entrepreneur

www.ingramcontent.com/pod-product-compliance
Lightning Source LLC
Chambersburg PA
CBHW070556170426
43201CB00012B/1859